Chartered Institute
Management Accountai

 C000291931

This book comes with free EN-gage online resources so that you can study anytime, anywhere. This free online resource is not sold separately and is included in the price of the book.

## How to access your online resources

You can access additional online resources associated with this CIMA Official book via the EN-gage website at: **www.EN-gage.co.uk/addabook**.

## Existing users

If you are an **existing EN-gage user**, simply log-in to your account using the address above, which will enable you to use the 'add a book' menu. Enter the ISBN of this book and the unique pass key number in the scratch panel below to gain access to the extra online products.

## New users

If you are a new EN-gage user then you will first need to register at: **www.EN-gage.co.uk**. Once registered, Kaplan Publishing will send you an email containing a link to activate your account - please check your junk mail if you do not receive this or contact us using the details printed on the back cover of this book. Click on the link to activate your account.

To unlock your additional resources, go to **www.EN-gage.co.uk/addabook**. You will then need to enter the ISBN of this book (found on page ii or the back cover) and the unique pass key number contained in the scratch panel below:

Then click 'finished' or 'add another book'.

Please allow 24 hours from the time you submit your book details for the content to appear in your account.

## Your code and information

This code can only be used once for the registration of one book online. This registration will expire when this edition of the book is no longer current - please see the back cover of this book for the expiry date.

## Using your online resources during your studies

All of the free online resources have been designed to supp-ort your studies. The extra online testing provides valuable question practice prior to your assessment and therefore we strongly recommend using this alongside this book.

# Managerial Level

# Subject P2

## Advanced Management Accounting

# EXAM PRACTICE KIT

CIMA
PUBLISHING

KAPLAN
PUBLISHING

Published by: Kaplan Publishing UK

Unit 2 The Business Centre, Molly Millars Lane, Wokingham, Berkshire RG41 2QZ

**British Library Cataloguing in Publication Data**

A catalogue record for this book is available from the British Library

ISBN: 978-1-78415-543-8

Printed and bound in Great Britain

# CONTENTS

|  | Page |
|---|---|
|
|

## Section

| | | |
|---|---|---|
|
|

Quality and accuracy are of the utmost importance to us so if you spot an error in any of our products, please send an email to mykaplanreporting@kaplan.com with full details.

Our Quality Co-ordinator will work with our technical team to verify the error and take action to ensure it is corrected in future editions.

# INDEX TO QUESTIONS AND ANSWERS

## OBJECTIVE TEST QUESTIONS

# EXAM TECHNIQUES

## COMPUTER-BASED ASSESSMENT

### TEN GOLDEN RULES

1   Make sure you have completed the compulsory 15 minute tutorial before you start exam. This tutorial is available through the CIMA website. You cannot speak to the invigilator once you have started.

2   These exam practice kits give you plenty of exam style questions to practise so make sure you use them to fully prepare.

3   Attempt all questions, there is no negative marking.

4   Double check your answer before you put in the final answer although you can change your response as many times as you like.

5   On multiple choice questions (MCQs), there is only one correct answer.

6   Not all questions will be MCQs – you may have to fill in missing words or figures.

7   Identify the easy questions first and get some points on the board to build up your confidence.

8   Try and allow 15 minutes at the end to check your answers and make any corrections.

9   If you don't know the answer, flag the question and attempt it later. In your final review before the end of the exam try a process of elimination.

10   Work out your answer on the whiteboard provided first if it is easier for you. There is also an onscreen 'scratch pad' on which you can make notes. You are not allowed to take pens, pencils, rulers, pencil cases, phones, paper or notes.

# SYLLABUS GUIDANCE, LEARNING OBJECTIVES AND VERBS

## A AIMS OF THE SYLLABUS

The aims of the syllabus are

- to provide for the Institute, together with the practical experience requirements, an adequate basis for assuring society that those admitted to membership are competent to act as management accountants for entities, whether in manufacturing, commercial or service organisations, in the public or private sectors of the economy

- to enable the Institute to examine whether prospective members have an adequate knowledge, understanding and mastery of the stated body of knowledge and skills

- to complement the Institute's practical experience and skills development requirements.

## B STUDY WEIGHTINGS

A percentage weighting is shown against each topic in the syllabus. This is intended as a guide to the proportion of study time each topic requires.

All component learning outcomes will be tested and one question may cover more than one component learning outcome.

The weightings do not specify the number of marks that will be allocated to topics in the examination.

## C LEARNING OUTCOMES

Each topic within the syllabus contains a list of learning outcomes, which should be read in conjunction with the knowledge content for the syllabus. A learning outcome has two main purposes:

1    to define the skill or ability that a well-prepared candidate should be able to exhibit in the examination

2    to demonstrate the approach likely to be taken by examiners in examination questions.

The learning outcomes are part of a hierarchy of learning objectives. The verbs used at the beginning of each learning outcome relate to a specific learning objective, e.g. Evaluate alternative approaches to budgeting.

The verb 'evaluate' indicates a high-level learning objective. As learning objectives are hierarchical, it is expected that at this level students will have knowledge of different budgeting systems and methodologies and be able to apply them.

A list of the learning objectives and the verbs that appear in the syllabus learning outcomes and examinations follows and these will help you to understand the depth and breadth required for a topic and the skill level the topic relates to.

| Learning objectives | Verbs used | Definition |
|---|---|---|
| **1 Knowledge** | | |
| What you are expected to know | List | Make a list of |
| | State | Express, fully or clearly, the details of/ facts of |
| | Define | Give the exact meaning of |
| **2 Comprehension** | | |
| What you are expected to understand | Describe | Communicate the key features of |
| | Distinguish | Highlight the differences between |
| | Explain | Make clear or intelligible/State the meaning of |
| | Identify | Recognise, establish or select after consideration |
| | Illustrate | Use an example to describe or explain something |
| **3 Application** | | |
| How you are expected to apply your knowledge | Apply | To put to practical use |
| | Calculate/compute | To ascertain or reckon mathematically |
| | Demonstrate | To prove with certainty or to exhibit by practical means |
| | Prepare | To make or get ready for use |
| | Reconcile | To make or prove consistent/ compatible |
| | Solve | Find an answer to |
| | Tabulate | Arrange in a table |
| **4 Analysis** | | |
| How you are expected to analyse the detail of what you have learned | Analyse | Examine in detail the structure of |
| | Categorise | Place into a defined class or division |
| | Compare and contrast | Show the similarities and/or differences between |
| | Construct | To build up or compile |
| | Discuss | To examine in detail by argument |
| | Interpret | To translate into intelligible or familiar terms |
| | Produce | To create or bring into existence |
| **5 Evaluation** | | |
| How you are expected to use your learning to evaluate, make decisions or recommendations | Advise | To counsel, inform or notify |
| | Evaluate | To appraise or assess the value of |
| | Recommend | To advise on a course of action |
| | Advise | To counsel, inform or notify |

# D OBJECTIVE TEST

The most common types of Objective Test questions are:

- multiple choice, where you have to choose the correct answer(s) from a list of possible answers. This could either be numbers or text.

- multiple choice with more choices and answers – for example, choosing two correct answers from a list of eight possible answers. This could either be numbers or text.

- single numeric entry, where you give your numeric answer e.g. profit is $10,000.

- multiple entry, where you give several numeric answers e.g. the charge for electricity is $2000 and the accrual is $200.

- true/false questions, where you state whether a statement is true or false e.g. external auditors report to the directors is FALSE.

- matching pairs of text e.g. the convention 'prudence' would be matched with the statement' inventories revalued at the lower of cost and net realisable value'.

- other types could be matching text with graphs and labelling graphs/diagrams.

In this Exam Practice Kit we have used these types of questions.

Some further guidance from CIMA on number entry questions is as follows:

- For number entry questions, you do not need to include currency symbols or other characters or symbols such as the percentage sign, as these will have been completed for you. You may use the decimal point but must not use any other characters when entering an answer (except numbers) so, for example, $10,500.80 would be input as 10500.80

- When expressing a decimal, for example a probability or correlation coefficient, you should include the leading zero (i.e. you should input 0.5 not .5)

- Negative numbers should be input using the minus sign, for example −1000

- You will receive an error message if you try to enter a character or symbol that is not permitted (for example a '£' or '%' sign)

- A small range of answers will normally be accepted, taking into account sensible rounding

**Guidance re CIMA On-Screen calculator:**

As part of the computer based assessment software, candidates are now provided with a calculator. This calculator is on-screen and is available for the duration of the assessment. The calculator is accessed by clicking the calculator button in the top left hand corner of the screen at any time during the assessment.

All candidates must complete a 15 minute tutorial before the assessment begins and will have the opportunity to familiarise themselves with the calculator and practise using it.

Candidates may practise using the calculator by downloading and installing the practice exam at http://www.vue.com/athena/. The calculator can be accessed from the fourth sample question (of 12).

Please note that the practice exam and tutorial provided by Pearson VUE at http://www.vue.com/athena/ is not specific to CIMA and includes the full range of question types the Pearson VUE software supports, some of which CIMA does not currently use.

The Objective Tests are ninety minute computer-based assessments comprising 60 compulsory questions, with one or more parts. CIMA is continuously developing the question styles within the system and you are advised to try the online website demo at www.cimaglobal.com, to both gain familiarity with assessment software and examine the latest style of questions being used.

# APPROACH TO REVISION

## Stage 1: Assess areas of strengths and weaknesses

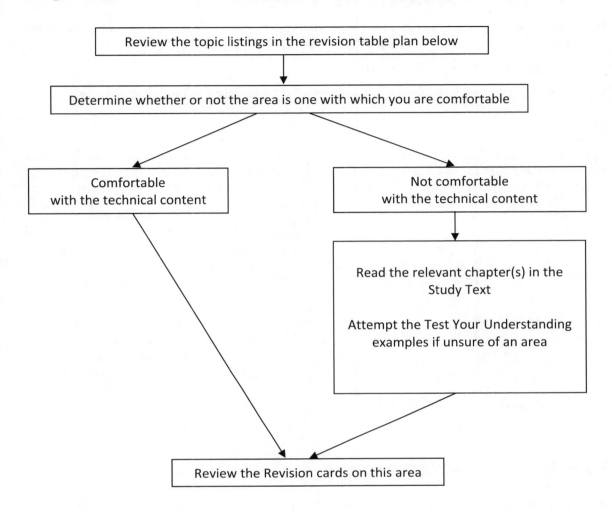

Review the topic listings in the revision table plan below

Determine whether or not the area is one with which you are comfortable

Comfortable
with the technical content

Not comfortable
with the technical content

Read the relevant chapter(s) in the
Study Text

Attempt the Test Your Understanding
examples if unsure of an area

Review the Revision cards on this area

## Stage 2: Question practice

Follow the order of revision of topics as recommended in the revision table plan below and attempt the questions in the order suggested.

Try to avoid referring to text books and notes and the model answer until you have completed your attempt.

Try to answer the question in the allotted time.

Review your attempt with the model answer and assess how much of the answer you achieved in the allocated exam time.

## Stage 3: Final pre-exam revision

We recommend that you **attempt at least one ninety minute mock examination** containing a set of previously unseen exam standard questions.

It is important that you get a feel for the breadth of coverage of a real exam without advanced knowledge of the topic areas covered – just as you will expect to see on the real exam day.

Ideally a mock examination offered by your tuition provider should be sat in timed, closed book, real exam conditions.

# P2
# ADVANCED MANAGEMENT ACCOUNTING

**Syllabus overview**

Focusing primarily on the long term, P2 builds on the insights about costs and their drivers (from P1) to provide the competencies needed to analyse, plan and manage costs to support the implementation of the organisation's strategy. It shows how to manage and control the performance of various units of the organisation in line with both short-term budgets and long-term strategy. Finally, P2 covers investment decision making and the risks associated with such decisions. It provides the basis for developing deeper understanding of various types of risk affecting the strategy and operations of organisations (covered in P3).

**Summary of syllabus**

| Weight | Syllabus topic |
|--------|----------------|
| 25% | A. Cost planning and analysis for competitive advantage |
| 30% | B. Control and performance management of responsibility centres |
| 30% | C. Long-term decision making |
| 15% | D. Management control and risk |

## P2 – A. COST PLANNING AND ANALYSIS FOR COMPETITIVE ADVANTAGE (25%)

**Learning outcomes**

On completion of their studies, students should be able to:

| Lead | Component | Indicative syllabus content |
|------|-----------|----------------------------|
| **1  evaluate techniques for analysing and managing costs for competitive advantage.** | (a)  evaluate activity-based management | <ul><li>Activity-based costing to derive 'long-run' costs appropriate for use in decision making.</li><li>Activity-based management and its use in improving the efficiency of repetitive overhead activities.</li><li>Direct and activity-based cost methods in tracing costs to 'cost objects', such as customers or distribution channels, and the comparison of such costs with appropriate revenues to establish 'tiered' contribution levels, as in the activity-based cost hierarchy.</li><li>Direct customer profitability and distribution channel profitability.</li></ul> |
| | (b)  evaluate total quality management (TQM) techniques | <ul><li>The impacts of just-in-time (JIT) production, the theory of constraints and total quality management on efficiency, inventory and cost.</li><li>The benefits of JIT production, total quality management and theory of constraints and the implications of these methods for decision making in the contemporary manufacturing environment.</li><li>Kaizen costing, continuous improvement and cost of quality reporting.</li><li>Process re-engineering and the elimination of non-value adding activities and reduction of activity costs.</li></ul> |
| | (c)  discuss techniques for enhancing long-term profits | <ul><li>Target costing and the determination of target costs from target prices.</li><li>Value analysis and quality function deployment.</li><li>The Value Chain and the management of contribution/profit generated throughout the chain.</li><li>Life cycle costing and its implications for marketing strategies.</li></ul> |

**Learning outcomes**
On completion of their studies, students should be able to:

| Lead | Component | Indicative syllabus content |
|------|-----------|------------------------------|
| | (d) apply learning curves to estimate time and cost for activities, products and services. | • Learning curves and their use in predicting product/service costs, including derivation of the learning rate and the learning index. |

## P2 – B. CONTROL AND PERFORMANCE MANAGEMENT OF RESPONSIBILITY CENTRES (30%)

**Learning outcomes**
On completion of their studies, students should be able to:

| Lead | Component | Indicative syllabus content |
|---|---|---|
| **1 discuss decision making in responsibility centres.** | (a) discuss the information needed for decision making in different organisational structures | • Relevant cost information for cost centre managers: controllable and uncontrollable costs and budget flexing.<br>• Relevant revenue and cost information for profit and investment centre managers: cost variability, attributable costs, controllable costs and identification of appropriate measures of profit centre 'contribution'.<br>• Alternative measures of performance for responsibility centres. |
| | (b) prepare reports to inform decisions. | • Performance reports: recognising issues of controllable/uncontrollable costs, variable/fixed costs and tracing revenues and costs to particular cost objects. |
| **2 discuss issues arising from the use of performance measures and budgets for control.** | (a) prepare performance reports for the evaluation of projected and actual performance | • Key metrics for the assessment of financial consequences including profitability, liquidity and asset turnover ratios, return on investment, residual income and economic value.<br>• Benchmarking.<br>• Analysis of reporting by dimension (e.g. segment, product, channel). |
| | (b) discuss traditional and non-traditional approaches to performance measurement | • Non-financial performance indicators.<br>• Balanced Scorecards (BSC). |
| | (c) discuss the criticisms and behavioural aspects of budgeting in responsibility centres. | • Behavioural issues in budgeting: participation in budgeting and its possible beneficial consequences for ownership and motivation; participation in budgeting and its possible adverse consequences for 'budget padding' and manipulation; setting budget targets for motivation; implications of setting standard costs etc.<br>• Criticisms of budgeting and the arguments for and against 'beyond budgeting'. |

**Learning outcomes**
On completion of their studies, students should be able to:

| Lead | Component | Indicative syllabus content |
|---|---|---|
| 3 **evaluate issues arising from the division of the organisation into responsibility centres.** | (a) discuss the likely behavioural consequences of performance measurement within an organisation | • The behavioural consequences of performance management and control in responsibility centres.<br>• The behavioural consequences arising from divisional structures: internal competition and internal trading. |
| | (b) discuss transfer pricing systems | • The theory of transfer pricing, including perfect, imperfect and no market for the intermediate good.<br>• Negotiated, market, cost-plus and variable cost-based transfer prices. Dual transfer prices and lump sum payments as means of addressing some of the issues that arise. |
| | (c) evaluate the effects of transfer prices. | • The motivation of divisional management.<br>• Divisional and group profitability.<br>• The autonomy of individual divisions. |

## P2 – C. LONG-TERM DECISION MAKING (30%)

**Learning outcomes**
On completion of their studies, students should be able to:

| Lead | Component | Indicative syllabus content |
|------|-----------|------------------------------|
| **1 evaluate information to support project appraisal.** | (a) analyse information for use in long-term decision making (including consideration of tax, inflation and other factors) | • Relevant cash flows taking account of tax, inflation and other factors, and the use of perpetuities to derive 'final' project value where appropriate.<br>• The identification and integration of non-financial factors in long-term decisions. |
| | (b) discuss the financial consequences of dealing with long-run projects, in particular the importance of accounting for the 'time value of money' | • The process of investment decision making, including origination of proposals, creation of capital budgets, go/no go decisions on individual projects (where judgements on qualitative issues interact with financial analysis).<br>• Discounting, including the use of annuities in comparing projects with unequal lives and the profitability index in capital rationing situations.<br>• Capital investment real options (i.e. to make follow-on investment, abandon or wait). |
| | (c) evaluate investment appraisal techniques and explain their results. | • The strengths and weaknesses of: payback, discounted payback, accounting rate of return (ARR), net present value (NPV), internal rate of return (IRR) and modified internal rate of return (based on a project's terminal value).<br>• Prioritisation of projects that are mutually exclusive, and/or are subject to single-period capital rationing, and/or have unequal lives. |
| **2 discuss pricing strategies and their consequences.** | (a) discuss pricing strategies and their consequences. | • Pricing decisions for profit maximising in imperfect markets. **Note :** Tabular methods of solution are acceptable.<br>• Pricing strategies and the financial consequences of market skimming, premium pricing, penetration pricing, loss leaders, product bundling/optional extras and product differentiation to appeal to different market segments. |

## P2 – D. MANAGEMENT CONTROL AND RISK (15%)

**Learning outcomes**
On completion of their studies, students should be able to:

| Lead | Component | Indicative syllabus content |
|---|---|---|
| **1 analyse information to assess its impact on long-term decisions.** | (a) apply sensitivity analysis | • Sensitivity analysis to identify the input variables that most affect the chosen measure of project worth (payback, ARR, NPV or IRR). |
| | (b) analyse risk and uncertainty. | • Quantification of risk.<br>• Probabilistic models and interpretation of distribution of project outcomes.<br>• Decision trees.<br>• Bayes Theorem.<br>• Decision making in conditions of uncertainty. |
| **2 discuss management's responsibilities with regard to risk.** | (a) discuss risk management | • Upside and downside risk.<br>• The TARA framework – transfer, avoid, reduce, accept.<br>• Business risks.<br>• Ethical implications and the public interest. |
| | (b) discuss the risks associated with the collection and use of information. | • Costs and benefits associated with investing in information systems.<br>• Big Data. |

# TABLES

Information concerning formulae and tables will be provided via the CIMA website, www.cimaglobal.com, and your ENgage login.

# Section 1

# OBJECTIVE TEST QUESTIONS

## A: COST PLANNING AND ANALYSIS FOR COMPETITIVE ADVANTAGE

1   EFG has recently introduced an activity-based costing system. It manufactures three products, details of which are set out below:

|  | Product E | Product F | Product G |
|---|---|---|---|
| Budgeted annual production (units) | 75,000 | 120,000 | 60,000 |
| Batch size (units) | 200 | 60 | 30 |
| Machine set-ups per batch | 5 | 3 | 9 |
| Purchase orders per batch | 4 | 2 | 2 |
| Processing time per unit (minutes) | 3 | 4 | 4 |

Three cost pools have been identified. Their budgeted costs for the year ending 30 September 20X3 are as follows:

| | |
|---|---|
| Machine set-up costs | $180,000 |
| Purchasing of materials | $95,000 |
| Processing | $110,000 |

**The budgeted machine set-up cost per unit of product F is nearest to:**

A   $0.17

B   $0.35

C   $0.76

D   $3.10

2   AB Company is a supermarket group that incurs the following costs:

(i)     The bought-in price of the good

(ii)    Inventory financing costs

(iii)   Shelf refilling costs

(iv)   costs of repacking or 'pack out' prior to storage before sale.

**AB Company's calculation of direct product profit (DPP) would include:**

A     All of the above costs

B     All of the above costs except (ii)

C     All of the above costs except (iv)

D     Costs (i) and (iii) only

**3**  A company sells five products. Sales data for the past year are as follows:

| Product | Sales Units | Sales price per unit $ |
|---|---|---|
| A | 2,000 | 25 |
| B | 1,000 | 40 |
| C | 6,000 | 5 |
| D | 5,000 | 20 |
| E | 10,000 | 2 |

**How would a Pareto analysis of sales revenue be presented, in a table format?**

A  In the order A, B, C, D, E

B  In the order D, A, B, C, E

C  In the order E, C, D, A, B

D  In the order B, A, D, C, E

**4**  M manufactures three products: A, B and C. Products A and B are manufactured in batches of ten units. Product C is a high-value product that is manufactured in single units.

In a typical month, production comprises 500 units of A, 400 of B and 20 of C. Product C is manufactured to order and it is very unusual for M to make more than one unit of C per day.

The quality control department has to inspect each unit produced. The department costs a total of $5,020 per month to run.

The monthly cost of running the quality control department is broken down as follows:

| | $ |
|---|---|
| Setting up test equipment | 2,200 |
| Inspection | 2,820 |

The test equipment has to be set up differently for each product. Once set up, the equipment can test up to ten units before it has to be recalibrated. The time and cost of setting up the equipment is the same for each product.

Each unit of A and B requires the same amount of time for inspection. Each unit of C requires twice as much inspection time. M has an activity-based management system.

**The cost per unit of quality control for each unit of C under an activity-based management approach is (in $, two decimal points):**

$ _____

**5**  **Kaizen costing emphasises:**

A  the need to achieve a target and maintain it

B  continuous improvement

C  the immediate elimination of all inefficiencies

D  Japanese culture

**6**   A bakery produces and sells a range of products. The following represents the results for the last month

| Product | Contribution |
|---|---|
| | $000 |
| Brown loaves | 67 |
| Family-sized cakes | 53 |
| Filled rolls | 26 |
| Individual cakes | 83 |
| Pasties and pies | 16 |
| Plain rolls | 42 |
| White loaves | 94 |

**Select ALL the statements that apply below:**

○   Pasties and Pies are the least profitable product.

○   Four of the product lines make up nearly 80% of the contribution for the bakery firm.

○   The most profitable products are bread and cakes.

○   White loaves outsell all other products, in value terms.

○   Management attention should be focused on bread and cakes, which represent 78% of the profitability of the bakery.

**7**   **Complete the following text by selecting the missing words and phrases (the same word may be used more than once):**

| activities | cost pools | cost | inspections |
|---|---|---|---|
| activity | quality inspection | driver | standards |
| multiple | single | factor | |

A cost _____ is any _____ that causes a change in the _____ of an _____, so the most important factor when selecting a _____ driver is to identify a *causal* relationship between the cost driver and the costs. Such a relationship may arise because of some physical relationship or because of the logic of the situation.

For example, _____ costs are caused by the action of carrying out an inspection to ensure quality _____ are being achieved, so the appropriate cost _____ would be the number of _____ carried out. Some _____ may have _____ cost drivers associated with them; in such a situation it is best if the costs can be analysed into separate _____ for each of which a _____ driver can be identified.

**8**   **X PLC**

X plc manufactures three products in a modern manufacturing plant, using cell operations. Budgeted output for April 2009 was

Product R 1,800 units in 36 batches

Product S 1,000 units in 10 batches

Product T 1,000 units in 40 batches

The product details are as follows:

| Product: | R | S | T |
|---|---|---|---|
| Standard labour hours per batch | 25 | 30 | 15 |
| Batch size (units) | 50 | 100 | 25 |
| Machine set-ups per batch | 3 | 2 | 5 |
| Power (kJ) per batch | 1.4 | 1.7 | 0.8 |
| Purchase orders per batch | 5 | 3 | 7 |
| Machine hours per batch | 10 | 7.5 | 12.5 |

During April 2009, the actual output was

Product R 1,500 units in 30 batches

Product S 1,200 units in 12 batches

Product T 1,000 units in 40 batches

The following production overhead budgetary control statement has been prepared for April 2009 on the basis that the variable production overhead varies in relation to standard labour hours produced.

**Production overhead budgetary control report April 2009**

| | Original budget | Flexed budget | Actual | Variances |
|---|---|---|---|---|
| Output (standard hours produced) | 1,800 | 1,710 | 1,710 | |
| | $000 | $000 | $000 | $000 |
| Power | 1,250 | 1,220 | 1,295 | 75 (A) |
| Stores | 1,850 | 1,800 | 1,915 | 115 (A) |
| Maintenance | 2,100 | 2,020 | 2,100 | 80 (A) |
| Machinery cleaning | 800 | 760 | 870 | 110 (A) |
| Indirect labour | 1,460 | 1,387 | 1,510 | 123 (A) |
| | 7,460 | 7,187 | 7,690 | 503 (A) |

After the above report had been produced, investigations revealed that every one of the individual costs could be classified as wholly variable in relation to the appropriate cost drivers.

**Budgeted cost per driver for each of the overhead costs, in $:**

Power: [                    ] per KJ

Stores: [                    ] per order

Maintenance: [                    ] per machine hour

Machinery cleaning: [                    ] per set-up

9   Having attended a CIMA course on activity-based costing (ABC) you decide to experiment by applying the principles to the four products currently made and sold by your company. Details of the four products and relevant information are given below for one period:

| Product | A | B | C | D |
| --- | --- | --- | --- | --- |
| Output in units | 120 | 100 | 80 | 120 |
| Costs per unit | $ | $ | $ | $ |
| Direct material | 40 | 50 | 30 | 60 |
| Direct labour | 28 | 21 | 14 | 21 |
| Machine hours (per unit) | 4 | 3 | 2 | 3 |

The four products are similar and are usually produced in production runs of 20 units and sold in batches of 10 units.

The production overhead is currently absorbed by using a machine hour rate, and the total of the production overhead has been analysed as follows:

|  | $ |
| --- | --- |
| Machine department costs (rent, business rates, depreciation and supervision) | 10,430 |
| Set-up costs | 5,250 |
| Stores receiving | 3,600 |
| Inspection/quality control | 2,100 |
| Material handling and dispatch | 4,620 |

You have ascertained that the 'cost drivers' to be used are as listed below for the overhead costs shown:

| Cost | Cost driver |
| --- | --- |
| Set-up costs | Number of production runs |
| Stores receiving | Requisitions raised |
| Inspection/quality control | Number of production runs |
| Materials handling and dispatch | Orders executed |

The number of requisitions raised on the stores was 20 for each product and the number of orders executed was 42, each order being for a batch of 10 of a product.

**If all overhead costs are absorbed on a machine hour basis total costs for each product are**

|  | Total costs in $ |
| --- | --- |
| Product A |  |
| Product B |  |
| Product C |  |
| Product D |  |

**If all overhead costs are absorbed using activity based costing, total costs for each product are**

|  | Total costs in $ |
| --- | --- |
| Product A |  |
| Product B |  |
| Product C |  |
| Product D |  |

**10**   S Company has been investigating the time taken to produce one of its products, and found that a 90% learning curve appears to be applicable.  If the time taken for the first unit is 7 hours, the total time taken in hours for units 5 to 8 only is:

A   17.078

B   18.144

C   19.590

D   20.142

**11**   A company has recently completed the production of the first unit of a new product. The time taken for this was 12 minutes. The company expects that there will be a 75% learning rate for this product.

**Calculate the total time expected to produce the first four units.**

**12**   FH is an electronics company that has developed a new product for the video conferencing market. The product has successfully completed its testing phase and FH has now produced the first four production units.

The first unit took three hours of labour time and the total time for the first four units was 8.3667 hours.

**Calculate the learning curve improvement rate (rate of learning) to the nearest 0.1%.**

**13**   PT has discovered that, when it employs a new test engineer, there is a learning curve with a 75% rate of learning that exists for the first 12 customer assignments. A new test engineer completed her first customer assignment in 6 hours.

**Calculate the time that she should take for her 7th assignment to the nearest 0.01 hours.**

**Note:** The index for a 75% learning curve is –0.415.

**14**   Q Company has developed a new product, the QX9.  The time taken to produce the first unit was 21 minutes.  Assuming that a 80% learning curve applies, the time allowed for the sixth unit (to 2 decimal places) should be:

A   5.24 minutes

B   8.25 minutes

C   11.65 minutes

D   11.80 minutes

**Note:** For an 80% learning curve $y = ax^{-0.3219}$

**15**   In the context of quality costs, customer compensation costs and test equipment running costs would be classified as:

|   | Customer compensation costs | Test equipment running costs |
|---|---|---|
| A | Internal failure costs | Prevention costs |
| B | Internal failure costs | Appraisal costs |
| C | External failure costs | Appraisal costs |
| D | External failure costs | Prevention costs |

**16** Which of the following are usually elements of a JIT system?

(i) Machine cells

(ii) Inventory only held at the bottleneck resource

(iii) Close relationship with major suppliers

(iv) Multi-skilled labour

A (i), (ii) and (iii) only

B (i), (iii) and (iv) only

C (i) and (iii) only

D All of these

**17** Which of the following statements about JIT is correct?

A JIT protects an organisation against risks of disruption in the supply chain.

B A narrow geographical spread in a business makes JIT more difficult to apply.

C With JIT, there is a risk that inventories could become obsolete.

D JIT is more difficult to implement when it is not easy to predict patterns of demand.

**18** Which of the following are aspects of a successful JIT system?

(i) Demand-driven production.

(ii) Savings in total machine set-up time.

(iii) Grouping machines or workers by product or component rather than by the type of work performed.

A (i) and (ii) only

B (i) and (iii) only

C (ii) and (iii) only

D All of these

**19** The following details relate to Product Z:

| | $/unit |
|---|---|
| Selling price | 45.00 |
| Purchased components | 14.00 |
| Labour | 10.00 |
| Variable overhead | 8.50 |
| Fixed overhead | 4.50 |
| | |
| Time on bottleneck resource | 10 minutes |

**Product return per minute is:**

A $0.80

B $1.25

C $2.10

D $3.10

**20**   A company manufactures four products – J, K, L and M. The products use a series of different machines but there is a common machine, X, which causes a bottleneck.

The standard selling price and standard cost per unit for each product for the forthcoming year are as follows:

|  | J | K | L | M |
|---|---|---|---|---|
|  | $ | $ | $ | $ |
| Selling price | 2,000 | 1,500 | 1,500 | 1,750 |
| *Cost:* |  |  |  |  |
| Direct materials | 410 | 200 | 300 | 400 |
| Labour | 300 | 200 | 360 | 275 |
| Variable overheads | 250 | 200 | 300 | 175 |
| Fixed overheads | 360 | 300 | 210 | 330 |
| Profit | 680 | 600 | 330 | 570 |
| Machine X – minutes per unit | 120 | 100 | 70 | 110 |

**Using a throughput accounting approach, the ranking of the products would be:**

|  | J | K | L | M |
|---|---|---|---|---|
| A | 1st | 2nd | 3rd | 4th |
| B | 1st | 2nd | 4th | 3rd |
| C | 2nd | 1st | 4th | 3rd |
| D | 2nd | 3rd | 1st | 4th |

**21**   **The selling price of product K is set at $450 for each unit and sales for the coming year are expected to be 600 units. If the company requires a return of 20% in the coming year on its investment of $300,000 in product K, the target cost for each unit for the coming year is:**

A    $300

B    $350

C    $400

D    $450

**22**   A company produces two products, S and T, which pass through two production processes, X and Y. The time taken to make each product in each process is:

|  | *Product S* | *Product T* |
|---|---|---|
| Process X | 5 mins | 7.5 mins |
| Process Y | 18 mins | 12 mins |

The company operates a 15-hour day and the processes have an average downtime each day of:

| Process X | 1.5 hours |
|---|---|
| Process Y | 1.0 hours |

The costs and revenue for each unit of each product are:

|  | Product S | Product T |
|---|---|---|
|  | $ | $ |
| Direct materials | 20.00 | 20.00 |
| Direct labour | 18.00 | 14.00 |
| Variable overhead | 4.00 | 4.00 |
| Fixed costs | 5.00 | 4.00 |
| Total cost | 48.00 | 42.00 |
| Selling price | $95.00 | $85.00 |

**Sales demand restricts the output of S and T to 50 and 80 units a day respectively. Calculate the daily production plan that would maximise the throughput contribution.**

23    NF Company has received an order to make 8 units of product C.  The time to produce the first unit is estimated to be 80 hours and an 80% learning curve is expected.  The rate of pay is $7.50 for each hour.

The direct material cost for each unit is $4,000 and the fixed costs associated with the order are $6,400.

**Calculate the average cost of each unit (to the nearest $) for this order of product K.**

24    BG has recently developed a new product. The nature of BG's work is repetitive, and it is usual for there to be an 80% learning effect when a new product is developed. The time taken for the first unit was 22 minutes.

**Assuming that an 80% learning effect applies, what is the time to be taken for the fourth unit?**

25    **In calculating the life cycle costs of a product, which of the following items would be excluded?**

(i)    Planning and concept design costs

(ii)    Preliminary and detailed design costs

(iii)    Testing costs

(iv)    Production costs

(v)    Distribution and customer service costs

A    (iii)

B    (iv)

C    (v)

D    None of them

**26** S Company manufactures accessories for the car industry. The following annual information regarding three of its key customers is available:

|  | J | H | K |
|---|---|---|---|
| Gross margin | $2,000,000 | $3,000,000 | $2,500,000 |
| General administration costs | $65,000 | $110,000 | $52,000 |
| Units sold | 20,000 | 32,000 | 27,500 |
| Orders placed | 1,500 | 1,500 | 2,000 |
| Sales visits | 156 | 172 | 208 |
| Invoices raised | 3,000 | 3,000 | 4,000 |

The company uses an activity-based costing system and the analysis of customer-related costs is as follows:

| Sales visits | $400 per visit |
|---|---|
| Order processing | $50 per order placed |
| Despatch costs | $150 per order placed |
| Billing and collections raised | $150 per invoice |

**Using customer profitability analysis, the ranking of the customers would be:**

|  | J | H | K |
|---|---|---|---|
| A | 1st | 2nd | 3rd |
| B | 1st | 3rd | 2nd |
| C | 2nd | 1st | 3rd |
| D | 3rd | 1st | 2nd |

**27** A company is changing its costing system from traditional absorption costing based on labour hours to an ABC system. It has overheads of $156,000 which are related to taking material deliveries.

The delivery information about each product is given below:

| Product | X | Y | Z |
|---|---|---|---|
| Total units required | 1,000 | 2,000 | 3,000 |
| Delivery size | 200 | 400 | 1,000 |

Total labour costs are $360,000 for 45,000 hours. Each unit of each product takes the same number of direct hours.

**Assuming that the company uses the number of deliveries as its cost driver, what is the increase or decrease in unit costs for Z arising from the change from AC to ABC?**

A $0.50 increase

B $0.50 decrease

C $14.00 increase

D $14.00 decrease

28 MB manufactures a product that requires 3.75 hours per unit of machining time. Machine time is a bottleneck resource, because there is a limited number of machines. There are just seven machines, and each is available for up to 15 hours each day, five days a week.

The product has a selling price of $100 per unit, a direct material cost of $40 per unit, a direct labour cost of $10 per unit and a factory overhead cost of $30 per unit. These costs are based on a weekly production and sales volume of 140 units.

**What is the throughput accounting ratio? (2 d.p.)**

29 **When building up the cost of a product or service using activity-based costing, which of the following would be used as levels of classification?**

(i) Facility

(ii) Product

(iii) Batch

(iv) Unit

(v) Value added

(vi) Non-value added

A (i) and (ii) only

B (ii), (iii) and (iv) only

C (i), (ii), (iii) and (iv)

D All of them

30 **Which of the following statements are correct?**

(i) A cost driver is any factor that causes a change in the cost of an activity.

(ii) For long-term variable overhead costs, the cost driver will be the volume of activity.

(iii) Traditional absorption costing tends to under-allocate overhead costs to low-volume products.

A (i) and (iii) only

B (ii) and (iii) only

C (i), (ii) and (iii)

D (i) only

31 RDE plc uses an activity-based costing system to attribute overhead costs to its three products. The following budgeted data relates to the year to 31 December 2008:

| Product | X | Y | Z |
|---|---|---|---|
| Production units (000) | 15 | 25 | 20 |
| Batch size (000 units) | 2.5 | 5 | 4 |

Machine set-up costs are caused by the number of batches of each product and have been estimated to be $600,000 for the year.

**Calculate the machine set-up costs that would be attributed to each unit of product Y:**

$ [                    ]

32    A food processing company operates an activity-based costing (ABC) system.  Which of the following would be classified as a facility-sustaining activity?

(i)      General staff administration

(ii)     Plant management

(iii)    Technical support for individual products and services

(iv)    Updating of product specification database

(v)     Property management

A      (i), (ii) and (v)

B      (ii), (iii) and (iv)

C      (ii), (iii), (iv) and (v)

D      All of them

33    The following data refers to a soft drinks manufacturing company that passes its product through five processes and is currently operating at optimal capacity.

| Process | Washing | Filling | Capping | Labelling | Packing |
|---|---|---|---|---|---|
| Time per unit | 6 mins | 3 mins | 1.5 mins | 2 mins | 6 mins |
| Machine hours available | 1,200 | 700 | 250 | 450 | 1,300 |

| Product data | $ per unit |
|---|---|
| Selling price | 0.60 |
| Direct material | 0.18 |
| Direct labour | 0.02 |
| Factory fixed cost | $4,120 |

Calculate:

The maximum output possible in the time available:

The throughput accounting ratio (2 d.p.):

34    A company developing a new product first makes a prototype for testing, secondly makes a demonstration model, and then begins production.  The time taken to make the prototype is 300 hours and, from past experience of similar models, it is known that a 90% learning curve applies.

The average time for the first two production models is (in hours):

35    The following statements have all been claimed to relate to the adoption of a TQM approach. Tick ALL that apply:

○    Employees should focus on the requirements of their customers, both internal and external.

○    Standard costing is unlikely to be used as a method of control.

○    TQM companies often dispense with the quality control department.

**36** **Which of the following costs are likely to be reduced on the introduction of a JIT system in a company? Tick ALL that apply:**

- ○ Purchasing costs
- ○ Inventory holding costs
- ○ Ordering costs
- ○ Information system costs

**37** **Which of the following statements relating to JIT and TQM approaches is most closely related to the truth?**

A    TQM and JIT are not very compatible approaches since their focus is different: one focuses on quality and the other on inventory levels.

B    TQM and JIT are not usually seen together since TQM is used by service companies and JIT by manufacturing companies.

C    TQM and JIT are very compatible approaches as they are both largely focused on customer satisfaction.

D    TQM and JIT are not compatible approaches since TQM requires there to be inventory so that quality checking can take place.

**38** **Which of the following is not a term normally used in value analysis?**

A    Resale value

B    Use value

C    Esteem value

D    Cost value

**39** **Which of the following is not suitable for a JIT production system?**

A    Batch production

B    Jobbing production

C    Process production

D    Service production

**40** Companies that embrace TQM often split their costs into four categories: prevention costs, appraisal costs, internal failure costs and external failure costs. A company wants to categorise the following costs:

(i)     Training staff in the importance of quality.

(ii)    Replacing, from inventory, a defective item returned by a customer.

(iii)   Scrapping an item deliberately tested to destruction.

(iv)    Losses on the sale of items identified as rejects.

**Which categories best reflect the nature of the above costs?**

|   | Prevention costs | Appraisal costs | Internal failure costs | External failure costs |
|---|---|---|---|---|
| A | (i) | (ii) | (iii) | (iv) |
| B | (i) | (iii) | (iv) | (ii) |
| C | (ii) | (iv) | (iii) | (i) |
| D | (iii) | (i) | (iv) | (ii) |

41   Complete the following text by selecting the missing words and phrases (the same word may be used more than once):

| reliability | cost | function | quality |
|---|---|---|---|
| value | quality inspection | driver | economically |
| relationships | functional | factors | reduction |

_____ analysis is an examination of the _____ affecting the cost of a product or service with the objective of achieving the specified purpose most _____at the required level of _____ and _____.

_____ analysis is an analysis of the _____ between product functions, the _____ of their provision and their perceived _____to the customer.

Therefore, _____ analysis is a form of cost _____ which is based upon investigating the processes involved in providing a product or service, whereas _____ analysis focuses on the value to the customer of each _____ of the product or service and from this determines whether it is necessary to reduce the cost of providing each function.

42   **Direct Product Profitability is most commonly found in:**

A   The car manufacturing industry

B   The grocery trade

C   Product design departments

D   The travel agency business

E   Production departments

**43** **Complete the following text by selecting the missing words and phrases (the same word may be used more than once):**

| internal | sequence | relationships | quality |
|----------|----------|---------------|---------|
| value | customers | distribution | value chain |
| products | suppliers | factors | chain |

The extended value _____ includes both _____ and external _____ whereas the _____ includes only the internal factors. The value chain is the _____of business _____that add _____ to the organisation's _____ and services and comprises the following:

— Research and Development (R&D)

— Design

— Production

— Marketing

— _____

— Customer service

The extended value chain adds _____ to the left hand side and _____ to the right hand side and recognises the importance of the _____ that the organisation has with these external parties in the overall process of adding value.

**44** **Complete the following text by selecting the missing words and phrases (the same word may be used more than once):**

| updated | reduction in stock levels | releases | several |
|---------|---------------------------|----------|---------|
| continuous improvement | customer lead | manufacturing | cellular |
| zero | high | reduction | target |

Just-in-Time, like so many modern management techniques, places great importance on the '_____' ethos. Cost containment will often aim to achieve a pre-determined _____, but this _____ may often remain static over a long period of time. With modern techniques, the target is regularly _____ and made more stringent.

Continual cost _____ can be seen in many areas of JIT:

- _____ – large amounts of capital is tied up in _____ stock levels. Reducing stock levels _____ this cash, so that it can be better used elsewhere in the business. Ideally, _____stock should be held.

- Reduction in _____ times and _____ times – the demand based manufacturing of JIT, together with _____manufacturing enables production times to be greatly reduced. This will improve customer satisfaction and hopefully lead to increased business volume.

- Cross-training of staff: new production methods necessitate staff being competent in _____ tasks. This may lead to fewer staff being required hence costs are reduced.

**45**   **Drag and drop the four following labels onto their appropriate definition:**

| Prevention costs | Appraisal costs | Internal failure costs | External failure costs |
|---|---|---|---|

| | |
|---|---|
| Costs associated with stopping the output of products which fail to conform to the specifications. | Costs of materials or products that fail to meet specifications |
| Costs arising when poor quality products are delivered to customers. | Costs associated with ensuring that production meets standards. |

**46**   A company has recently adopted throughput accounting as a performance measuring tool. Its results for the last month are shown below.

| | | |
|---|---|---|
| Units produced | | 1,150 |
| Units sold | | 800 |
| Materials purchased | 900 kg costing | $13,000 |
| Opening material inventory used | 450 kg costing | $7,250 |
| Labour costs | | $6,900 |
| Overheads | | $4,650 |
| Sales price | | $35 |

There were no opening inventory of finished goods or closing inventory of materials.

**What is the throughput accounting ratio for this product? (2 d.p.)**

**47**   A company is considering the price that it should charge for a repeat order. Fifteen units of the product have already been made and supplied to the customer and the company has experienced an 80% learning curve so far. The first unit required 54 hours of labour to complete the manufacture, assembly and testing processes.

**Assuming that the 80% learning curve continues, calculate the expected time to be taken for the 16th unit.**

**Note:** The learning index for an 80% learning curve is – 0.3219.

**48**   The times taken to produce each of the first four batches of a new product were as follows:

| Batch number | Time taken |
|---|---|
| 1 | 100 minutes |
| 2 | 70 minutes |
| 3 | 61 minutes |
| 4 | 58 minutes |

**Based upon the above data, the rate of learning was closest to:**

A   85.0%

B   78.6%

C   70.0%

D   69.3%

**49** A company is preparing a quotation for a new product. The time taken for the first unit of the product was 30 minutes and the company expects an 85% learning curve. The quotation is to be based on the time taken for the final unit within the learning period which is expected to end after the company has produced 200 units.

**Calculate the time per unit to be used for the quotation.**

**Note:** The learning index for an 85% learning curve is −0.2345.

**50** The 'materials handling' business process of Company A consists of the following activities: materials requisitioning, purchases requisitioning, processing purchase orders, inspecting materials, storing materials and paying suppliers. This process could be re-engineered by sending the materials requisitions directly to an approved supplier, and entering into an agreement which entails delivering high quality materials in accordance with production requirements.

**Which of the following cost reductions would be expected after re-engineering the materials handling process? Select ALL that apply.**

(i) Cost reduction due to the elimination of the administration involved in placing orders.

(ii) Cost reduction due to the elimination of the need for material inspection.

(iii) Cost reduction due to the elimination of the need for material storage.

A (i) only

B (i) and (ii) only

C (ii) and (iii) only

D All of them

**51** **What attempts to move away from a traditional hierarchic organisation structure, in order to respond to the demands of a customer service-oriented business environment, where quality is the key strategic variable?**

A Business Process Re-engineering

B Total Quality Management

C Continuous Process Improvement

D Business Process Management

## B: CONTROL AND PERFORMANCE MANAGEMENT OF RESPONSIBILITY CENTRES

**52**  Division P is an investment centre within PC Ltd. Over which of the following is the manager of Division P likely to have control?

(I)  Transfer prices

(ii)  Level of inventory in the division

(iii)  Discretionary fixed costs incurred in the division

(iv)  Apportioned head office costs

A  (i), (ii), (iii) and (iv)

B  (i), (ii) and (iii) only

C  (i) and (ii) only

D  (i) only

**53**  **Within decentralised organisations, there may be cost centres, investment centres and profit centres. Which of the following statements is true?**

A  Cost centres have a higher degree of autonomy than profit centres

B  Investment centres have the highest degree of autonomy and cost centres the lowest

C  Investment centres have the lowest degree of autonomy

D  Profit centres have the highest degree of autonomy and cost centres the lowest

**54**  A company makes three products xx, yy and zz. The following information is available

|  | XX | YY | ZZ |
|---|---|---|---|
|  | $ | $ | $ |
| Sales | 18,000 | 40,000 | 68,000 |
| Variable costs | 10,000 | 35,000 | 48,000 |
| Fixed costs | 5,000 | 9,000 | 14,000 |
| Profit/(Loss) | 3,000 | (4,000) | 6,000 |

It is believed that a percentage of the fixed costs relating to product YY are avoidable.

**What is the minimum percentage of fixed costs that must be avoidable if the company is to cease producing product YY? (Calculate to the nearest whole percentage.)**

**55    HULME**

Hulme has three divisions. Budgeted information for the forthcoming period is as follows:

|  | Division T | Division H | Division E | Total |
|---|---|---|---|---|
|  | $000 | $000 | $000 | $000 |
| Sales | 700 | 560 | 150 | 1,410 |
| Variable costs | (550) | (440) | (100) | (1,090) |
| Contribution | 150 | 120 | 50 | 320 |
| Fixed costs |  |  |  | 450 |
| Profit |  |  |  | (130) |

Eighty per cent of the fixed costs are specific to each division being split between T, H and E in the ratio 3:4:1, respectively.

Which divisions should be kept open by Hulme given that their objective is to maximise profit?

**56    X PLC**

X plc intends to use relevant costs as the basis of the selling price for a special order: the printing of a brochure. The brochure requires a particular type of paper that is not regularly used by X plc although a limited amount is in X plc's inventory which was left over from a previous job.

The cost when X plc bought this paper last year was $15 per ream and there are 100 reams in inventory. The brochure requires 250 reams. The current market price of the paper is $26 per ream, and the resale value of the paper in inventory is $10 per ream.

**What is the relevant cost of the paper to be used in printing the brochure?**

$ [                    ]

**57**    T plc manufactures a component D12, and two main products F45 and P67. The following details relate to each of these items:

|  | D12 | F45 | P67 |
|---|---|---|---|
|  | $ per unit | $ per unit | $ per unit |
| Selling price | – | 146.00 | 159.00 |
| Material cost | 10.00 | 15.00 | 26.00 |
| Component D12 (bought-in price) | – | 25.00 | 25.00 |
| Direct labour | 5.00 | 10.00 | 15.00 |
| Variable overheads | 6.00 | 12.00 | 18.00 |
| Total variable cost per unit | 21.00 | 62.00 | 84.00 |

| Fixed overhead costs: | $ per annum | $ per annum | $ per annum |
|---|---|---|---|
| Avoidable* | 9,000 | 18,000 | 40,000 |
| Non-avoidable | 36,000 | 72,000 | 160,000 |
| Total | 45,000 | 90,000 | 200,000 |

\* The avoidable fixed costs are product-specific fixed costs that would be avoided if the product or component were to be discontinued.

**Assuming that the annual demand for component D12 is 5,000 units and that T plc has sufficient capacity to make the component itself, what is the maximum price that should be paid to an external supplier for 5,000 components per year?**

**Assuming that component D12 is bought from an external supplier for $25.00 per unit, what number of units of product F45 that must be sold to cover its own costs without contributing to T plc's non-avoidable fixed costs?**

58 You are currently in employment earning $25,000 per annum. You have decided to go into business for yourself doing PC repairs for local companies and will operate out of a unit available for rent at the edge of the town.

**How should (i) your current salary and (ii) the rent of the unit be treated when deciding whether or not to start the business?**

A (i) as an irrelevant cost and (ii) as an opportunity cost

B (i) as a sunk cost and (ii) as an committed cost

C (i) as an incremental cost and (ii) as an opportunity cost

D (i) as a committed cost and (ii) as a sunk cost

E (i) as an opportunity cost and (ii) as an incremental cost

59 **RIGHTLIGHT LTD**

Rightlight Ltd is an advertising company and has been asked to tender for a contract to increase public awareness of global environmental issues as part of the government's commitment to improving the country's eco-footprint.

Rightlight Ltd believes that the campaign work will take a period of six months.

Five advertising specialists would need to be recruited on an annual salary of $45,000. A project manager would be needed to coordinate the campaign. An existing project manager would be used whose annual salary is currently $55,000. He would be expected to devote 30% of his time on the new contract.

The new employees would have to go through a 'Environmental Awareness' training programme in order to get approval to work on government contracts. This would cost $3,000 per employee, but it is anticipated that a grant of 20% towards this cost will be available.

Alternatively, Rightlight Ltd could subcontract the work (with the government's agreement) to another PR that it sometimes uses for joint venture projects. It is anticipated that the subcontract firm would demand a fee of $135,000 to undertake the work.

**What would be the relevant cost of labour for this contract?**

$ _____

**60** A service company evaluates its performance using a number of key ratios. This includes the current ratio which is targeted not to fall below a value of 2.

Forecasts to date predict that receivables will fluctuate between $135,000 and $142,000, and payables between $17,000 and $22,000. The company has no inventory.

**What is the maximum budgeted overdraft permitted if the company is to achieve its target?**

$ [          ]

**61** **A division has a return on investment of 18% and an asset turnover of two times. What is the division's net profit margin?**

**62** **An organisation is divided into a number of divisions, each of which operates as a profit centre. Which of the following would be useful measures to monitor divisional performance?**

(i)     Contribution

(ii)    Controllable profit

(iii)   Return on investment

(iv)    Residual income

(v)     Economic value added

A     (i) only

B     (i) and (ii) only

C     (iii), (iv) and (v) only

D     All of them

**63** A company evaluates its performance using a number of key ratios. This includes the current ratio which is targeted not to fall below a value of 1.7.

Forecasts for the elements of working capital are inventory $14,800, receivables $19,600 and payables $144,000.

**What is the minimum budgeted bank balance permitted if the company is to achieve its target?**

$ [          ]

**64** **A division has a net profit margin of 16% and an asset turnover of 0.9 times. What is the division's return on investment?**

**65** **A company has an asset turnover of 5 and a net profit margin of 4%. It has profits of $80,000. What is the value of its capital employed?**

$ [          ]

**66** Extracts from B's master budget for the latest period are as follows:

| Income statement | $000 |
|---|---|
| Revenue | 5,440 |
| Gross profit | 2,730 |
| Profit from operations | 900 |
| **Balance sheet** | |
| Non-current assets | 1,850 |
| Inventory | 825 |
| Receivables | 710 |
| Bank | 50 |
| Current liabilities | 780 |

**Calculate the following figures:**

The operating profit margin for the budget period ☐ %

The total net asset turnover for the period ☐ times (2 d.p.)

The budgeted current ratio ☐ times (2 d.p.)

The budgeted quick (acid test) ratio ☐ times (2 d.p.)

**67   DB HOLDINGS LTD**

You have been asked to comment on the financial position of DB Holdings Ltd. You have obtained copies of the two most recent sets of the company's audited accounts which are summarised as follows:

| All figures in $000 | 2013 | 2014 |
|---|---|---|
| Equipment net of depreciation | 2,400 | 2,200 |
| Premises | 1,600 | 900 |
| Inventory | 560 | 1,080 |
| Receivables | 320 | 980 |
| Cash/(Overdraft) | 160 | −180 |
| Payables | −280 | −780 |
| | | |
| Net assets | 4,760 | 4,200 |
| Share capital | 1,600 | 1,600 |
| Loan from Directors | 2,200 | 1,400 |
| Cumulative retained profits | 960 | 1,200 |
| | | |
| Capital | 4,760 | 4,200 |
| Revenue (sales) | 4,800 | 5,800 |
| Operating profit | 320 | 420 |
| Dividends paid | 80 | 180 |

You know that due to the nature of the company's business, most of its business costs are purchases. The chairman of DB Holdings has recently quoted in the press:

DB Holdings has always been a profitable company. However, we are following a high growth strategy and this has put pressure on cash flow. We have a number of new clients signed up and believe the future is bright.

**Calculate the following business metrics for DB Holdings Ltd. in 2013 (first column) and 2014 (second column)**

| | | |
|---|---|---|
| ROCE | | |

| | | |
|---|---|---|
| Profit margin on sales | | |

| | | |
|---|---|---|
| Receivables days | | |

| | | |
|---|---|---|
| Inventory days | | |

| | | |
|---|---|---|
| Payables days | | |

| | | |
|---|---|---|
| Cash conversion period | | |

68  A company has set a target ROI of 12% for its divisions, this is deemed to represent the return necessary to benefit the company.

Division D achieved an ROI of 17% last year and is not expecting any major change from ongoing operations.

The purchase of a new piece of equipment has been proposed by a member of the production team. It is estimated that it will boost profits by $128,000 per annum for an investment of $855,000.

**Is the divisional manager likely to accept or reject the investment? Will this be to the benefit or the detriment of the company?**

69  A company has set a target ROI of 14% for its divisions, this is based on the company's cost of capital.

Division D achieved an ROI of 8% last year and is not expecting any major change from ongoing operations. However, a manager has suggested that cost savings of $15,000 per annum can be obtained by investing $135,000 in upgrading a particular piece of equipment.

**Is the divisional manager likely to accept or reject the investment? Will this be to the benefit or the detriment of the company?**

70  A company uses ROI to assess divisional performance, but it is considering switching to RI. The company's cost of capital is 15%.

Division C has an ROI of 21% which is not expected to change. An investment of $155,000 is available, which is expected to yield profits of $28,000 per annum.

**Is the manager of division C likely to accept or reject the investment if ROI is used to assess performance? Would this change if RI was used?**

**71** Division G of a large company is approaching its year end. The division is evaluated using ROI with a target rate of return of 15%. The division has control of all aspects of its operation except that all cash balances are centralised by the company and therefore left off divisional balance sheets.

The divisional manager is considering the following options.

(i) To delay payment of a supplier until next year, the potential prompt payment discount of 5% will be lost. The debt is for $27,500.

(ii) To scrap a redundant asset with a book value of $147,000. The manager has been offered $15,000 as immediate scrap proceeds, whilst he is fairly confident that he could get $25,000 in an industry auction to be held at the start of the new year.

**Assume that the manager is very short-termist (i.e. only considers the implications for this year) and that the expected ROI for the year, before these options, is 18%. Which of the following represents the most likely combination that the manager will choose?**

|   | (i) | (ii) |
|---|---|---|
| A | Delay | Scrap now |
| B | Delay | Scrap next year |
| C | Do not delay | Scrap now |
| D | Do not delay | Scrap next year |

**72** A divisionalised company uses transfer pricing as part of its management information system. Each manager is assessed on their divisional profit.

Division A makes a unit for $10 variable cost and $3 of fixed cost is absorbed.

Division B takes these units, incurs another $8 variable cost and absorbs $4.

It then sells them for $21.

The transfer price is set at $12.

There are no capacity constraints and all fixed costs are unavoidable in the short run.

**Select ALL that apply:**

○ The manager of division A is likely to produce the units.

○ The manager of divisions B is likely to produce the units.

○ From the company's perspective, production should occur.

○ The transfer price is goal congruent.

**73** **Which of the following is NOT a method of transfer pricing?**

A Cost plus transfer price

B Internal price

C Market-based transfer price

D Two part transfer price

**74**   TM plc makes components which it sells internally to its subsidiary RM Ltd, as well as to its own external market.

   **The external market price is $24.00 per unit, which yields a contribution of 40% of sales. For external sales, variable costs include $1.50 per unit for distribution costs, which are not incurred on internal sales. TM plc has sufficient capacity to meet all of the internal and external sales. In order to maximise group profit, at what unit price should the component be transferred to RM Ltd?**

   $ [_____]

**75**   Division A makes alphas which are converted into betas by division B. A's variable costs are $150 per unit and B's are $80 per unit. B sells completed betas for $290 each. There is an intermediate market for alphas with a price of $180 which significantly exceeds the capacity of divisions A and B.

   **(i)**   **Assuming that B cannot buy from the market in alphas (but A can sell into the market), what is the widest range of TP that encourages the divisions to trade with each other?**

   $ [_____]       to       $ [_____]

   **(ii)**   **Assuming that A cannot sell into the market in alphas (but B can buy from the market), what is the widest range of TP that now encourages the divisions to trade with each other?**

   $ [_____]       to       $ [_____]

**76**   **One of the main reasons for adopting a decentralised organisation in preference to a centralised organisation structure is the:**

   A   improved goal congruence between the divisional manager's goals and the goals of the organisation

   B   availability of less subjective measures of performance

   C   improved communication of information among the organisation's managers

   D   rapid response of management to environmental changes

**77** A company has the following balance sheet totals at the end of its most recent financial year:

|                               | $million |
|-------------------------------|----------|
| Non-current assets            | 3.64     |
| Current assets                | 0.42     |
| Share capital and reserves*   | 2.69     |
| Long-term debt                | 1.00     |
| Current liabilities           | 0.37     |

\* Includes retained profit for the year of $320,000 after deducting:

| Ordinary share dividends      | $200,000 |
| Interest on long-term debt    | $100,000 |
| Taxation                      | $70,000  |

Calculate, to 1 d.p., the Return On Investment (ROI) of the company for the year (using end-year balance sheet values for investment).

 %

**78** A division of a company has capital employed of $2m and its return on capital is 12%. It is considering a new project requiring capital of $500,000 and is expected to yield profits of $90,000 per annum. The company's interest rate is 10%. If the new project is accepted, the residual income of the division will be:

A $40,000

B $80,000

C $30,000

D $330,000

**79** Division M has produced the following results in the last financial year:

|                    |                      | $000  |
|--------------------|----------------------|-------|
| Net profit         |                      | 360   |
| Capital employed:  | Non-current assets   | 1,500 |
|                    | Net current assets   | 100   |

For evaluation purposes all divisional assets are valued at original cost.

The division is considering a project which will increase annual net profit by $25,000, but will require average inventory levels to increase by $30,000 and non-current assets to increase by $100,000.

There is an 18% capital charge on investments.

Given these circumstances, will the evaluation criteria of Return on Investment (ROI) and Residual Income (RI) motivate Division M management to accept this project?

|   | ROI | RI  |
|---|-----|-----|
| A | Yes | Yes |
| B | Yes | No  |
| C | No  | Yes |
| D | No  | No  |

**80**   Summary financial statements are given below for one division of a large divisionalised company.

Summary divisional financial statements for the year to 31 December

| *Balance sheet* | | *Income statement* | |
|---|---|---|---|
| | $000 | | $000 |
| Non-current assets | 1,500 | Revenue | 4,000 |
| Current assets | 600 | Operating costs | 3,600 |
| | | | |
| Total assets | 2,100 | Operating profit | 400 |
| | | Interest paid | 70 |
| | | | |
| Divisional equity | 1,000 | Profit before tax | 330 |
| Long-term borrowings | 700 | | |
| Current liabilities | 400 | | |
| | | | |
| Total equity and liabilities | 2,100 | | |

**The cost of capital for the division is estimated at 12% each year. Annual rate of interest on the long-term loans is 10%. All decisions concerning the division's capital structure are taken by central management. The divisional Return on Investment (ROI) for the year ended 31 December is:**

A    19.0%

B    19.4%

C    23.5%

D    33.0%

**81**   Summary financial statements are given below for one division of a large divisionalised company.

Summary divisional financial statements for the year to 31 December

| Balance sheet | | Income statement | |
|---|---|---|---|
| | $000 | | $000 |
| Non-current assets | 1,500 | Revenue | 4,000 |
| Current assets | 600 | Operating costs | 3,600 |
| | | | |
| Total assets | 2,100 | Operating profit | 400 |
| | | Interest paid | 70 |
| | | | |
| Divisional equity | 1,000 | Profit before tax | 330 |
| Long-term borrowings | 700 | | |
| Current liabilities | 400 | | |
| | | | |
| Total equity and liabilities | 2,100 | | |

The cost of capital for the division is estimated at 12% each year.

Annual rate of interest on the long-term loans is 10%.

All decisions concerning the division's capital structure are taken by central management.

**The divisional Residual Income (RI) for the year ended 31 December is:**

A     $160,000

B     $196,000

C     $230,000

D     $330,000

**82**    A division has net assets of $420,000. The profit statement for the division for the latest period is as follows:

|  | $ |
| --- | --- |
| Revenue | 630,000 |
| Variable costs | 390,000 |
| Contribution | 240,000 |
| Attributable fixed costs | 180,000 |
| Allocated central costs | 25,000 |
| Divisional profit | 35,000 |

The divisional manager is considering investing in a machine costing $50,000. The machine would earn annual profits, after depreciation, of $5,500. The company's cost of capital is 10%.

**Calculate the division's controllable return on investment, without the new machine:**

                                                  %

**Calculate the division's controllable return on investment, with the new machine:**

                                                  %

**Calculate the controllable residual income for the division with the new machine:**

$

**Calculate the controllable residual income for the division without the new machine:**

$

**83** An investment centre has earned an accounting profit of $135,000, after charging historical cost depreciation of $22,000 and increasing the provision for doubtful debts by $8,000 to $12,000. If the non-current assets had been valued at replacement cost the depreciation charge would have been $41,000.

The net book value of the investment centre's net assets is $420,000 and the replacement cost is estimated to be $660,000. The organisation's risk adjusted cost of capital is 14% but it has a large bank loan which incurs annual interest charges of 10%.

**Ignoring taxation, the economic value added (EVA) for the investment centre is:**

A    $29,920

B    $31,040

C    $31,600

D    $56,800

**84** Division G has reported annual operating profits of $20.2 million. This was after charging $3 million for the full cost of launching a new product that is expected to last three years.

Division G has a risk adjusted cost of capital of 11% and is paying interest on a substantial bank loan at 8%. The historical cost of the assets in Division G, as shown on its balance sheet, is $60 million, and the replacement cost has been estimated at $84 million.

Ignore the effects of taxation.

**What would be the EVA for Division G?**

A    $15.4 million

B    $11.48 million

C    $10.6 million

D    $12.74 million

**85** The following data have been extracted from a company's year-end accounts:

|                        | $         |
|------------------------|-----------|
| Turnover               | 7,055,016 |
| Gross profit           | 4,938,511 |
| Operating profit       | 3,629,156 |
| Non-current assets     | 4,582,000 |
| Cash at bank           | 4,619,582 |
| Short term borrowings  | 949,339   |
| Trade receivables      | 442,443   |
| Trade payables         | 464,692   |

**Calculate the following four performance measures:**

(i)    Operating profit margin

(ii)   Return on capital employed

(iii)  Trade receivable days (debtors days)

(iv)   Current (Liquidity) ratio.

**86** **Which of the following best describes an investment centre?**

A    A centre for which managers are accountable only for costs.

B    A centre for which managers are accountable only for financial outputs in the form of generating sales revenue.

C    A centre for which managers are accountable for profit.

D    A centre for which managers are accountable for profit and current and non-current assets.

**87** ABC has two profit centres, Centre 1 and Centre 2. Centre 1 transfers one third of its output to Centre 2 and sells the remainder on the external market for $28 per unit. The transfers to Centre 2 are at a transfer price of cost plus 20%.

Centre 2 incurs costs of $8 per unit in converting the transferred unit, which is then sold to external customers for $40 per unit. Centre 1 costs are $20 per unit and the budgeted output for period 6 is 450 units. There is no budgeted change in inventories for either profit centre.

**The budgeted results for Centre 1 and Centre 2 for period 6 will be:**

|   | Centre 1 | Centre 2 |
|---|---|---|
| A | $1,800 profit | $2,400 profit |
| B | $3,000 profit | $1,200 profit |
| C | $3,000 profit | $4,800 profit |
| D | $3,900 profit | $2,400 profit |

**88** **Which of the following statements about market-based transfer prices are correct?**

(i)    A profit centre buying the item is likely to be indifferent between buying externally and buying the item from within the business.

(ii)    A transfer price at market value might not encourage profit centres buying the item to utilise spare capacity.

A    (i) only

B    (ii) only

C    Both (i) and (ii)

D    Neither (i) nor (ii)

**89** X plc, a manufacturing company, has two divisions: Division A and Division B. Division A produces one type of product, ProdX, which it transfers to Division B and also sells externally. Division B has been approached by another company which has offered to supply 2,500 units of ProdX for $35 each. The following details for Division A are available:

|  | $ |
|---|---|
| Sales revenue | |
| Sales to Division B @ $40 per unit | 400,000 |
| External sales @ $45 per unit | 270,000 |
| *Less:* | |
| Variable cost @ $22 per unit | 352,000 |
| Fixed costs | 100,000 |
| Profit | 218,000 |

External sales of Prod X cannot be increased, and division B decides to buy from the other company.

**The annual (increase/reduction)\* in divisional profit for Division A amounts to:**

$ [                    ]

**The annual (increase/reduction)\* in profit for Company X amounts to:**

$ [                    ]

(*) Delete as appropriate

**90** X and Y are two divisions of Newtyle. Division X manufactures one product, Alpha. Unit production cost and market price are as follows:

|  | $ |
|---|---|
| Direct materials | 6 |
| Direct labour | 4 |
| Fixed overhead | 1 |
|  | 11 |
| Prevailing market price | $16 |

Product Alpha is sold outside the company in a perfectly competitive market and also to Division Y. If sold outside the company, Alpha incurs variable selling costs of $2 per unit which are not incurred on internal transfers.

**If the total demand for Alpha were more than sufficient for Division X to manufacture to capacity, at what price would the company prefer Division X to transfer Alpha to Division Y?**

A    $10

B    $11

C    $14

D    $16

**91** Division A transfers 100,000 units of a component to Division B each year. The market price of the component is $25 per unit.

Division A's variable cost is $15 per unit. Its fixed costs are $500,000 each year.

**What price per unit would be credited to Division A for each component that it transfers to Division B under marginal cost pricing and under two-part tariff pricing (where the Divisions have agreed that the fixed fee will be $200,000)?**

| | Marginal cost pricing | Two-part tariff pricing |
|---|---|---|
| A | $15 | $15 |
| B | $25 | $15 |
| C | $15 | $25 |
| D | $25 | $25 |

**92** Division S transfers 75,000 units of a component to Division T each year. The market price of the component is $40. Division S's variable cost is $28 per unit. Division S's fixed costs are $380,000 each year.

**What price would be credited to Division S for each component that it transfers to Division T under:**

(a) Two-part tariff pricing (where the Divisions have agreed that the fixed fee will be $160,000)?

(b) Dual pricing (based on marginal cost and market price)?

| | Two-part tariff pricing | Dual pricing |
|---|---|---|
| A | $12 | $28 |
| B | $12 | $40 |
| C | $28 | $40 |
| D | $33 | $28 |

**93** CD Globes transferred 11,000 units of product N from its manufacturing division in Canada to its selling division in the UK during the year just ended.

The manufacturing cost of each unit of product N was $120 (75% of which was variable cost). The market price for each unit of product N in Canada was $300. The Canada division's profit after tax for its sales to the UK division for the year ended was $1,100,000.

The UK division incurred marketing and distribution costs of £40 for each unit of product N and sold the product for £250 a unit. The UK tax rate was 25%. (Exchange rate: £1 = $1.50)

**If product N had been transferred at the Canadian market price, the tax rate in Canada must have been (to the nearest percentage point):**

A    32%

B    36%

C    40%

D    44%

**94** CD Globes transferred 11,000 units of product N from its manufacturing division in Canada to its selling division in the UK during the year just ended.

The manufacturing cost of each unit of product N was $120 (75% of which was variable cost). The market price for each unit of product N in Canada was $300. The Canada division's profit after tax for its sales to the UK division for the year ended was $1,100,000.

The UK division incurred marketing and distribution costs of £40 for each unit of product N and sold the product for £250 a unit. The UK tax rate was 25%. (Exchange rate: £1 = $1.50)

**If the transfers had been made at variable cost, the UK division's profit after tax would have been:**

A    £950,000

B    £987,500

C    £1,050,000

D    £1,237,500

**95** CMW Ltd is a UK holding company with an overseas subsidiary. The directors of CMW Ltd wish to transfer profits from the UK to the overseas company.

They are considering changing the level of transfer prices charged on goods shipped from the overseas subsidiary to CMW Ltd and the size of the royalty payments paid by CMW Ltd to its subsidiary.

**In order to transfer profit from CMW Ltd to the overseas subsidiary, the directors of CMW Ltd should:**

A    Increase both the transfer prices and royalty payments

B    Increase the transfer prices but decrease royalty payments

C    Decrease the transfer prices but increase royalty payments

D    Decrease both the transfer prices and royalty payments

**96** WX has two divisions, Y and Z. The following budgeted information is available.

Division Y manufactures motors and budgets to transfer 60,000 motors to Division Z and to sell 40,000 motors to external customers.

Division Z assembles food mixers and uses one motor for each food mixer produced.

The standard cost information per motor for Division Y is as follows:

|                                           | $   |
|-------------------------------------------|-----|
| Direct materials                          | 70  |
| Direct labour                             | 20  |
| Variable production overhead              | 10  |
| Fixed production overhead                 | 40  |
| Fixed selling and administration overhead | 10  |
|                                           | ——— |
| Total standard cost                       | 150 |
|                                           | ——— |

In order to set the external selling price the company uses a 33.33% mark up on total standard cost.

Calculate:

**The budgeted profit/(loss) for Division Y if the transfer price is set at marginal cost:**

$ [                    ]

**The budgeted profit/(loss) for Division Y if the transfer price is set at the total production cost:**

$ [                    ]

**97** The KL Company provides legal and secretarial services to small businesses. KL has two divisions.

*Secretarial Division*

This division provides secretarial services to external clients and to the Legal Division. It charges all its clients, including the Legal Division, at a rate of $40 per hour. The marginal cost of one hour of secretarial services is $20.

*Legal Division*

The Legal Division provides legal services. One service, called L&S, involves a combination of legal and secretarial services. Each hour of L&S charged to clients involves one hour of legal services and one hour of secretarial services. The secretarial element of this service is purchased from the Secretarial Division. The likely demand for L&S at different prices is as follows:

| Demand (hours) | Price per hour ($) |
|---|---|
| 0 | 100 |
| 1,000 | 90 |
| 2,000 | 80 |
| 3,000 | 70 |
| 4,000 | 60 |
| 5,000 | 50 |

The marginal cost of one hour of legal services is $25.

**Calculate the level of sales (hours) and total contribution of L&S that would maximise the profit from this service FOR THE LEGAL DIVISION. Assume the Legal Division pays the Secretarial Division at a rate of $40 per hour for secretarial services.**

[                    ] hours (level of sales)

[                    ] contribution

**Calculate the level of sales (hours) and total contribution that would maximise the profit from L&S FOR THE KL COMPANY AS A WHOLE.**

[                    ] hours (level of sales)

[                    ] contribution

**98**     The annual operating statement for a company is shown below:

|                      | $000   |
| -------------------- | ------ |
| Sales revenue        | 800    |
| Less variable costs  | 390    |
|                      |        |
| Contribution         | 410    |
| Less fixed costs     | 90     |
| Less depreciation    | 20     |
|                      |        |
| Net income           | 300    |

Assets                                                    $6.75m

**The cost of capital is 13% per annum. The return on investment (ROI) for the company is closest to:**

A     4.44%

B     4.74%

C     5.77%

D     6.07%

**99**     The annual operating statement for a company is shown below:

|                      | $000   |
| -------------------- | ------ |
| Sales revenue        | 800    |
| Less variable costs  | 390    |
|                      |        |
| Contribution         | 410    |
| Less fixed costs     | 90     |
| Less depreciation    | 20     |
|                      |        |
| Net income           | 300    |

Assets                                                    $6.75m

The cost of capital is 13% per annum.

**The residual income (RI) for the company is closest to (in $000):**

A     (467)

B     (487)

C     (557)

D     (577)

**100** A company has reported annual operating profits for the year of $89.2m after charging $9.6m for the full development costs of a new product that is expected to last for the current year and two further years. The cost of capital is 13% per annum. The balance sheet for the company shows fixed assets with a historical cost of $120m. A note to the balance sheet estimates that the replacement cost of these fixed assets at the beginning of the year is $168m. The assets have been depreciated at 20% per year.

The company has a working capital of $27.2m.

**Ignore the effects of taxation. The Economic Value Added (EVA) of the company is closest to:**

A    $64.16m

B    $70.56m

C    $83.36m

D    $100.96m

**101** ZP plc operates two subsidiaries, X and Y. X is a component-manufacturing subsidiary and Y is an assembly and final product subsidiary. Both subsidiaries produce one type of output only. Subsidiary Y needs one component from subsidiary X for every unit of Product W produced. Subsidiary X transfers to Subsidiary Y all of the components needed to produce Product W. Subsidiary X also sells components on the external market.

The following budgeted information is available for each subsidiary:

|  | X | Y |
|---|---|---|
| Market price per component | $800 | |
| Market price per unit of W | | $1,200 |
| Production costs per component | $600 | |
| Assembly costs per unit of W | | $400 |
| Non production fixed costs | $1.5m | $1.3m |
| External demand | 10,000 units | 12,000 units |
| Capacity | 22,000 units | |
| Taxation rates | 25% | 30% |

The production cost per component is 60% variable. The fixed production costs are absorbed based on budgeted output.

X sets a transfer price at marginal cost plus 70%.

**Calculate the post-tax profit generated by each subsidiary.**

**102** **Pick TWO strengths of using Return on Investment as a performance measure for Investment appraisal:**

○    It is an absolute measure of increase in shareholder wealth

○    It is commonly used and understood

○    It uses objective profits instead of subjective cash flows

○    It leads to goal congruent decisions

○    It cannot be manipulated

○    It can be used to compare projects of different sizes

103 **Division X's performance is based on return on investment (ROI) calculated using figures controllable by the division. Calculate, to 2 decimal places, the ROI % for division X based on the following figures:**

Net profit $675,000; Capital employed $10m

Included in net profit are:

Depreciation on division X's assets of $200,000

Depreciation on head office assets of $250,000

Financing costs of $100,000 to represent division X's share of a loan taken out by the company to restructure its financing structure.

104 **The following statements have been made with regards to the Return On Investment measure.**

Select ALL that apply:

(i) Projects with a return on investment that beats the company's cost of capital should always be accepted

(ii) Return on investment is a useful tool for evaluating profit centres

(iii) Return on investment is best calculated using profit after tax

(iv) Return on investment can be broken down into secondary measures of performance

105 A divisional manager currently earning a return on investment (ROI) of 18% is offered a project with the following cash flows:

Purchase of machinery: $600,000

Revenue: $20000 per month

Variable costs: $5,000 per month

Life of project: 5 years

Sale of machinery at end of project: $100,000

**The manager is evaluated on their ability to improve ROI. Based on the ROI the manager will achieve after 1 year of the project (assuming all other divisional activities carry on generating a ROI of 18%), should the project be accepted?**

**Select the correct answer below:**

A Yes, because the project return is greater than the company's cost of capital

B Yes, because the project ROI is 36%, which is greater than the current return

C Yes, because the project makes a profit over its life

D No, because the project ROI is 16% which is lower than the current return

**106** A new division has the following figures in relation to its first year:

Annual cash flows: $20,000

Assets invested at start of year: $50,000

Residual value: $5,000

Depreciation policy for assets: Straight line over 5 years

**Calculate the return on investment earned by the division as at the end of its first year to the nearest whole %**

```

```

**107** **Pick TWO strengths of using Residual Income as a performance measure for a large organisation/group:**

Option 1 It brings home the cost of financing to the divisional manager

Option 2 It is commonly used and understood

Option 3 It uses objective profits instead of subjective cash flows

Option 4 It often leads to goal congruent decisions

Option 5 It cannot be manipulated

Option 6 It can be used to compare divisions of different sizes within the division within a

**108** A division currently has an annual return on investment (ROI) of 20% on its investment base of $1,200,000. The following additional projects are being considered:

| Project | Investment outlay, in $000 | Annual profit in $000 | ROI% |
|---|---|---|---|
| A | 300 | 100 | 33 |
| B | 700 | 210 | 30 |
| C | 500 | 130 | 26 |
| D | 200 | 44 | 22 |

**Which combination of investments will maximise the division's return on investment, assuming no capital rationing is in place?**

A    All four projects

B    A, B  and C only

C    A and B only

D    A only

**109** A divisional manager currently earning a return on investment of 15% is offered a project with the following cash flows:

Purchase of machinery: $100,000      Revenue: $7,500 per month

Variable costs: $4,900 per month      Life of project: 5 years

Sale of machinery at end of project: $10,000      Depreciation method: straight line

The divisional manager's bonus is based on the Residual Income achieved by the division and is senior enough to influence the manager's decisions. The company's cost of capital is 12%.

**Would the manager accept this project?**

A      No, because the project has a negative Residual Income

B      Yes, because the project has a positive Residual Income

C      Yes, because the project makes a profit over its life

D      No, because the Return on Investment is 13.2% and is less than the division's current Return on Investment

**110** **The following statements have been made in relation to ROI and RI. Select ALL that apply:**

(i)      Residual income will always increase when investments earning a return higher than the cost of capital is undertaken.

(ii)      Return on investment will always increase when investments earning a return higher than the cost of capital are undertaken.

(iii)      Using residual income as a performance measure allows easy comparison between divisions.

(iv)      Return on investment will artificially increase over time if net book values of assets are included in the calculation of capital employed.

**111** **Calculate the controllable Residual Income (to the nearest $000) of division J (an investment centre) based on the following figures in ($'000):**

| | |
|---|---|
| Gross profit | 1,000 |
| Operating expenses | 600 (see note 1) |
| Net profit | 400 |
| Interest | 50 (see note 2) |
| Profit before tax | 350 |
| Tax | 25 (see note 2) |
| Profit after tax | 325 |

Note 1: within operating expenses is included $250,000 as a share of head office expenses, made up of an administration recharge of $100,000 and depreciation of $150,000.

Note 2: both interest and tax are calculated at company level and apportioned appropriately to the divisions

Capital employed by J:

Net assets      3,000

Net assets comprise the division J factory, worth $2m, and the division J office (which is an allocated floor of head office) worth $1m. The cost of capital of the company is 20%.

**112** A divisional manager is offered 2 projects:

Project A: Invest $50,000 to upgrade production machinery to be more efficient. The current net book value of the machinery is $1 million.

Contribution earned should increase by 20% from its current level of $100,000 per annum.

The upgrade will last for 4 years after which the machinery will be scrapped for $0 and replaced with new machinery.

Project B: Invest $1.5 million to buy a patent that will allow an upgraded version of the current product to be sold. Revenue per annum will increase from $1m per annum to $1.5m.

Variable costs will be 60% of revenue. Company policy is to capitalise patents and depreciate them on a straight line basis over their useful lives. The patent will lapse after 50 years.

**The company cost of capital is 13%. What decision will the divisional manager take if divisional evaluated based on residual income?**

A    Accept both projects

B    Reject both projects

C    Accept A and reject B

D    Accept B and reject A

**113** **Why would a company want to encourage the use of non-financial performance indicators?**

A    To encourage short-termism

B    To look at the fuller picture of the business

C    To enable results to be easily manipulated to the benefit of the manager

D    To prevent goal congruence

**114** **Complete the following text by selecting the missing words and phrases (the same word may be used more than once):**

| all | profitability | cost | returning customers |
|---|---|---|---|
| income from new products | non-financial | customer satisfaction | innovation and learning |
| efficiency | internal business | financial | survival |

The balanced scorecard approach is a way of providing information to management which involves the inclusion of _____information alongside financial information.

It emphasises the need to provide the user with a set of information which addresses _____relevant areas of performance in an objective and unbiased fashion.

Although the specific measures used may vary, a scorecard would normally include the following measures

- _____ – the financial perspective

- _____ – the customer perspective

- innovation – the _____ perspective

- internal efficiency – the _____ perspective.

By providing all this information in a single report, management is able to assess the impact of particular actions on all perspectives of the company's activities. Under each perspective, a company should state its aims and specify measures of performance.

For example:

| | | *Aims* | *Measure* |
|---|---|---|---|
| 1 | Financial perspective | _____ | Current ratio |
| 2 | Customer perspective | Satisfaction | _____ |
| 3 | Internal business perspective | _____ | Throughput rates |
| 4 | Innovation and learning | New products | _____ |

**115** **Which ONE of the following is not a perspective that is monitored by the Balanced Scorecard approach to performance measurement?**

A    Financial

B    Customer

C    Supplier

D    Innovation and learning

**116** **The following statements have been made about performance measures. Select ALL that apply:**

(i)    If a company uses a balanced scorecard approach to provide information, it will not use ROI or Residual Income as divisional performance measures.

(ii)    The residual income will always increase when investments earning above the cost of capital are undertaken.

(iii)    The internal business perspective of the Balanced Scorecard approach to the provision of information is concerned only with the determination of internal transfer prices that will encourage goal congruent decisions.

(iv)    An advantage of the residual income performance measure is that it facilitates comparisons between investment centres.

**117** Complete the following text by selecting the missing words and phrases (the same word may be used more than once):

| benchmarks | profitability | devolved | World-class performance |
|---|---|---|---|
| Management model | centralised | devolved networks | goals |
| adaptative | responsibility | financial | replace |

Beyond Budgeting (BB) is the name given to a body of practices intended to _____ budgeting as a _____. The core concept is the need to move from a business model based on _____organisational hierarchies to one based on_____.

BB is a '_____ model' whereby managers are given _____ which are based on _____ linked variously to _____, peers, competitors and/or earlier periods. This requires an _____ approach whereby authority is _____ to managers.

**118** A and B are two divisions of a company. A makes two products, Product A and Product B. Product A is commercialised outside the company. Product B is only sold to Division B, at a unit transfer price of $176. Unit costs for Product B are as follows:

|  | $ |
|---|---|
| Variable materials | 60 |
| Variable labour | 40 |
| Variable overheads | 40 |
| Fixed overheads | 20 |
|  | **160** |

Division B has received an offer from another company to supply a substitute for Product B, for $152 per unit.

**Assuming Division A can sell as much of Product A as it can produce and the unit profitability of Products A and B are equal, what will be the effects on profits if Division B accepts the offer?**

A     Profit in Division A would not change and the overall company profit would decrease.

B     Profit in Division A would decrease and the overall company profit would not change.

C     Profit in Division A would not change and the overall company profit would increase.

D     Profit in Division A would increase and the overall company profit would not change.

**119** U plc uses Return on Investment (ROI) to assess its divisional performance. U plc estimates that the net cash flows associated with a new piece of machinery will be equal in each of the five years of the asset's life, but the company's figures for capital employed and accounting profit have come under scrutiny.

**Which methods of stating these two components of ROI will provide figures which are constant from year to year over the five year life of this new asset?**

|   | *Capital employed* | *Accounting profit* |
|---|---|---|
| A | Gross book value | Profit after charging depreciation on a reducing balance basis |
| B | Gross book value | Profit after charging depreciation on a straight line basis |
| C | Net book value | Profit after charging depreciation on a straight line basis |
| D | Net book value | Profit after charging depreciation on a reducing balance basis |

**120** In order to regain a competitive position the Managing Director of MCG plc, a divisionalised business, has been advised to reduce the range of products and the product lines by about 20% to increase profits by at least 40%. To implement such a product divestment strategy could, he fears, alienate customers. He needs to know which products need to be removed and which products are important to the survival of the company. He is unhappy about the overall performance of his company's activities. Benchmarking has been recommended as a method of assessing how his company's performance compares with that of his competitors.

**Select ALL that apply:**

○ **Internal bench-marking** can compare different divisions within MCG: some centres may be more profitable than others.

○ **Internal benchmarking could result in** a transfer of knowledge and skills and could be beneficial to the group as a whole.

○ **Competitive benchmarking** attempts to compare products, processes and results and show where the company is failing with reference to those of competitors.

○ **Customer benchmarking** attempts to compare corporate performance with the performance expected by customers.

# C: LONG-TERM DECISION MAKING

**121** The details of an investment project are as follows:

| | |
|---|---|
| Cost of asset bought at the start of the project | $80,000 |
| Annual cash inflow | $25,000 |
| Cost of capital, after tax | 5% each year |
| Life of the project | 8 years |

Corporation tax is 25% and is paid in equal quarterly instalments in the 6th and 9th months of the year in which the profit was earned and in the 1st and 3rd months of the following year.

Writing down allowances of 20% reducing balance will be claimed each year.

(Assume the asset is bought on the first day of the tax year and that the company's other projects generate healthy profits.)

**The present value of the cash flows that occur in the *second year* of the project is:**

A    $17,006

B    $19,053

C    $20,271

D    $25,940

**122** A company is considering investing in a project that would have a four-year life span. The investment would involve an immediate cash outflow of $250,000 and have a zero residual value. In each of the four years, 6,000 units would be produced and sold. The contribution per unit, based on current prices, is $12. The company has an annual cost of capital of 10%. It is expected that the inflation rate will be 4% in each of the next four years.

**The net present value of the project (to the nearest $100) is:**

A    $800

B    $1,300

C    $1,800

D    $2,300

**123** B Company is deciding whether to launch a new product. The initial outlay for the product is $60,000. The forecast possible annual cash inflows and their associated probabilities are shown below:

| | Probability | Year 1 | Year 2 | Year 3 |
|---|---|---|---|---|
| Optimistic | 0.25 | $35,000 | $40,000 | $32,000 |
| Most likely | 0.55 | $20,000 | $26,000 | $28,000 |
| Pessimistic | 0.20 | $18,000 | $24,000 | $22,000 |

The company's cost of capital is 8% per annum.

Assume the cash inflows are received at the end of the year and that the cash inflows for each year are independent.

**The expected net present value for the product is:**

A ($500)

B $8,634

C $10,189

D $12,348

**124** A company is considering investing in a manufacturing project that would have a three-year life span. The investment would involve an immediate cash outflow of $50,000 and have a zero residual value. In each of the three years, 4,000 units would be produced and sold. The contribution per unit, based on current prices, is $5. The company has an annual cost of capital of 8%. It is expected that the inflation rate will be 3% in each of the next three years.

**The net present value of the project (to the nearest $500) is:**

A $4,500

B $5,000

C $5,500

D $6,000

**125** JAH Company is about to invest $400,000 in machinery and other capital equipment for a new product venture. Cash flows for the first three years are estimated as follows:

| Year | $000 |
|---|---|
| 1 | 210 |
| 2 | 240 |
| 3 | 320 |

JAH Company requires a 17% return for projects of this type. The above cash flows do not include expenditure on an advertising campaign, which will be incurred in equal annual amounts at the beginning of years 1, 2 and 3.

**Ignoring any residual values of the capital equipment, calculate the maximum annual amount that can be spent on advertising, to the nearest $000.**

$ [                    ]

**126**  X Company takes on a five-year lease of a building for which it pays $27,200 as a lump sum payment. X Company then sub-lets the building for five years at a fixed annual rent, with the rent payable annually in arrears.

**Calculate (to the nearest $) the annual rental charge, if the rent is set at a level that will earn a DCF yield of 17% for X Company.**

$ [                    ]

**127**  A company is evaluating a new product proposal. The proposed product selling price is $180 per unit and the variable costs are $60 per unit. The incremental cash fixed costs for the product will be $160,000 per annum. The discounted cash flow calculation results in a positive NPV:

|  |  | Cash flow $ | Discount rate | Present value $ |
|---|---|---|---|---|
| Year 0 | Initial outlay | (1,000,000) | 1.000 | (1,000,000) |
| Years 1–5 | Annual cash flow | 320,000 | 3.791 | 1,213,120 |
| Year 5 | Working capital released | 50,000 | 0.621 | 31,050 |
| Net present value |  |  |  | 244,170 |

**What is the percentage change in selling price (to 1 d.p.) that would result in the project having a net present value of zero?**

[                    ] %

**128**  A company is considering investing in a project that requires an initial outflow of $500,000 and will generate expected cash inflows in terms of today's $ of $130,000 over each of the next four years. The company's monetary cost of capital is 7% and inflation is predicted to be 4% over the next four years.

**Calculate:**

**The company's real cost of capital (2 d.p.)**

[                    ] %

**The net present value of the project, when discounting money cash flow at the money rate:**

$ [                    ]

**The net present value of the project, when discounting real cash flow at the real rate:**

$ [                    ]

**129**  **If the money discount rate is 12% and the real rate is 6%, what is the rate of inflation?**

A     5.66%

B     6.30%

C     18.60%

D     17.66%

**130**  The details of an investment project are:

| | |
|---|---|
| Life of the project | 10 years |
| Cost of asset bought at the start of the project | $100,000 |
| Annual cash inflow | $20,000 |
| Cost of capital, after tax | 8% each year |

Corporation tax is 30% and is paid in equal quarterly instalments in the 7th and 10th months of the year in which the profit was earned and in the 1st and 4th months of the following year.

Writing down allowances of 25% reducing balance will be claimed each year.

(Assume the asset is bought on the first day of the tax year and that the company's other projects generate healthy profits. Round all cash flows to the nearest $ and discount end of year cash flows.)

**Calculate the present value of the cash flows that occur in the second year of the project:**

$ [                    ]

**131**  **An investment project that requires an initial investment of $500,000 has a residual value of $130,000 at the end of five years. The project's cash flows have been discounted at the company's cost of capital of 12% and the resulting net present value is $140,500. The profitability index of the project is closest to:**

A  0.02

B  0.54

C  0.28

D  0.26

**132**  CC Company is considering an investment of $300,000 which will earn a contribution of $40,000 each year for 10 years at today's prices.  The contribution will rise at the rate of 6% per year because of inflation.  The company's cost of money is 11% per annum.

**The net present value of the project is**

$ [                    ]

**133**  A company has determined that the net present value of an investment project is $12,304 when using a 10% discount rate and $(3,216) when using a discount rate of 15%.

**The internal rate of return of the project, to the nearest 1%, is**

[                    ] %

**134** An investment project with no residual value has a net present value of $87,980 when it is discounted using a cost of capital of 10%. The annual cash flows are as follows:

| Year | $ |
|---|---|
| 0 | (200,000) |
| 1 | 80,000 |
| 2 | 90,000 |
| 3 | 100,000 |
| 4 | 60,000 |
| 5 | 40,000 |

**Calculate the Internal Rate of Return (IRR) of the project:**

**135** A company is to spend $60,000 on a machine that will have an economic life of ten years, and no residual value. Depreciation is to be charged using the straight-line method. Estimated operating cash flows are:

| Year | $ |
|---|---|
| 1 | −2,000 |
| 2 | 13,000 |
| 3 | 20,000 |
| 4–6 | 25,000 each year |
| 7–10 | 30,000 each year |

**What is the average accounting of return (ARR), calculated as average annual profits divided by the average investment?**

A    75%

B    55%

C    38%

D    28%

**136** **For a company with the objective of maximising net present value, what is the validity of the following statements for a conventional investment project?**

(i)    The accounting rate of return (ARR) method of project appraisal usually gives too little weight to cash flows which occur late in the project's life.

(ii)   For a project with a (unique) IRR greater than the opportunity cost of capital, the IRR method of project appraisal usually gives too little weight to cash flows which occur late in the project's life.

| | Statement 1 | Statement 2 |
|---|---|---|
| A | True | True |
| B | True | False |
| C | False | False |
| D | False | True |

**137** M plc is evaluating three possible investment projects and uses a 10% discount rate to determine their net present values.

| Investment | A | B | C |
|---|---|---|---|
| | $000 | $000 | $000 |
| Initial investment | 400 | 450 | 350 |
| | | | |
| Incremental cash flows | | | |
| Year 1 | 100 | 130 | 50 |
| Year 2 | 120 | 130 | 110 |
| Year 3 | 140 | 130 | 130 |
| Year 4 | 120 | 130 | 150 |
| Year 5* | 100 | 130 | 100 |
| | | | |
| Net present value | 39 | 55 | 48 |

* Includes $20,000 residual value for each investment project.

**Calculate the payback period of investment A:**

**Calculate the discounted payback period of investment B:**

**Calculate the Internal Rate of Return (IRR) of investment C:**

**138** X is considering the following five investments:

| Investment | J | K | L | M | N |
|---|---|---|---|---|---|
| | $000 | $000 | $000 | $000 | $000 |
| Initial investment | 400 | 350 | 450 | 500 | 600 |
| Net present value | 125 | 105 | 140 | 160 | 190 |

Investments J and L are mutually exclusive; all of the investments are divisible and none of them may be invested in more than once.

**The optimum investment plan for X assuming that the funding available is limited to $1m is:**

A    $400,000 in J plus $600,000 in N

B    $400,000 in M plus $600,000 in N

C    $500,000 in M plus $500,000 in N

D    $350,000 in K plus $600,000 in N plus $50,000 in M

**139** X ltd can choose from five mutually exclusive projects. The projects will each last for one year only, and their net cash inflows will be determined by the prevailing market conditions. The forecast annual cash inflows and their associated possibilities are shown below:

| Market conditions | Poor | Good | Excellent |
|---|---|---|---|
| Probability | 0.20 | 0.50 | 0.30 |
| | $000 | $000 | $000 |
| Project L | 500 | 470 | 550 |
| Project M | 400 | 550 | 570 |
| Project N | 450 | 400 | 475 |
| Project O | 360 | 400 | 420 |
| Project P | 600 | 500 | 425 |

**Based on the expected value of the cash inflows, which project should be undertaken?**

A    L

B    M

C    N

D    O

E    P

**140** A company is considering an investment of $400,000 in new machinery. The machinery is expected to yield incremental profits over the next five years as follows:

| Year | Profit ($) |
|---|---|
| 1 | 175,000 |
| 2 | 225,000 |
| 3 | 340,000 |
| 4 | 165,000 |
| 5 | 125,000 |

Thereafter, no incremental profits are expected and the machinery will be sold. It is company policy to depreciate machinery on a straight line basis over the life of the asset. The machinery is expected to have a value of $50,000 at the end of year 5.

**Calculate the payback period of the investment in this machinery to the nearest 0.1 years.**

**141** An investment company is considering the purchase of a commercial building at a cost of $0.85m. The property would be rented immediately to tenants at an annual rent of $80,000 payable in arrears in perpetuity.

**What is the net present value of the investment, assuming that the investment company's cost of capital is 8% per annum?**

Ignore taxation and inflation.

$ [                    ]

**142** Huron Ltd wishes to expand its operations. Six possible capital investments have been identified, but Huron only has access to a total of $570,000. The projects have unequal lives, are not divisible and may not be postponed. The following information is available (all calculations are correct and the cash outlays are given in $000):

| Project | Outlay in Year | NPV | Profitability Index |
|---|---|---|---|
| A | (246) | $6,350 | 0.026 |
| B | (180) | $1,882 | 0.010 |
| C | (175) | $(2,596) | –0.015 |
| D | (180) | $8,294 | 0.046 |
| E | (180) | $5,490 | 0.031 |
| F | (150) | $4,993 | 0.033 |

Projects A and E are mutually exclusive. All projects are believed to be of similar risk to the company's existing capital investments.

**Which combination of projects should be selected?**

A      D, E and F

B      A, B and F

C      A, D and F

D      A, D and E

**143** A machine costs $20,000. The following information is also available:

Running costs (payable at the end of the year) amount to $5,000 at the end of year 1. If the machine was kept on for another year, running costs would amount to $5,500 at the end of that year.

If the machine was disposed of after 1 year, the trade-in allowance would amount to $16,000. For a disposal after 2 years, the trade-in allowance would amount to $13,000

**Calculate the optimal replacement cycle if the cost of capital is 10%. The machine should be replaced after ......**

| | year(s) |
|---|---|

**144** **A decision has to be made on replacement policy for vans. A van costs $12,000, and the following additional information applies:**

| Van is sold at the end of year... | Trade-in allowance | Van kept in business for.... | Maintenance cost at the end of the year |
|---|---|---|---|
| 1 | $9,000 | 1 year | $0 |
| 2 | $7,500 | 2 years | $1,500 in the first year |
| 3 | $7,000 | 3 years | $2,700 in the second year |

The cost of capital is 15%. Vans are only maintained at the end of the year if they are to be kept for a further year, i.e. there are no maintenance costs in the year of replacement.

**Ignore taxation and inflation. Calculate the optimal replacement policy. Each van should be replaced after......**

| | year(s) |
|---|---|

**145** A machine costing $150,000 has a useful life of eight years, after which time its estimated resale value will be $30,000. Annual running costs will be $6,000 for the first three years of use and $8,000 for each of the next five years. All running costs are payable on the last days of the year to which they relate. Using a discount rate of 20% per annum, what is the equivalent annual cost (to the nearest $100) of using the machine, if it were bought and replaced every eight years in perpetuity?

    A    $21,100

    B    $34,000

    C    $30,400

    D    $44,200

**146** Pumpkin Ltd is considering purchasing a new machine at a cost of $110,400 that will be operated for four years, after which time it will be sold for an estimated $9,600. Pumpkin uses a straight line depreciation policy. Forecast operating profits to be generated by the machine are as follows:

| Year | $ |
|---|---|
| 1 | 39,600 |
| 2 | 19,600 |
| 3 | 22,400 |
| 4 | 32,400 |

What is the payback period ('PP') and the average accounting rate of return (ARR), calculated as average annual profits divided by the average investment?

    A    PP: 2.01 years ARR: 47.5%

    B    PP: 3.89 years ARR: 25.8%

    C    PP: 3.89 years ARR: 47.5%

    D    PP: 2.01 years ARR: 25.8%

**147** A company is currently evaluating a project which requires investments of $12,000 now, and $4,800 at the end of year 1. the cash inflow from the project will be $16,800 at the end of year 2 and $14,400 at the end of year 3. The cost of capital is 15%. Select the discounted payback period (DPP) and the net present value (NPV).

    A    DPP: 2.00 years NPV: $6,000

    B    DPP: 2.36 years NPV: $4,440

    C    DPP: 2.00 years NPV: $4,440

    D    DPP: 2.36 years NPV: $6,000

**148** Which of the following is not an advantage of the IRR?

    A    It considers the whole life of a project

    B    It uses cash flows not profits

    C    It is a measure of absolute return

    D    It considers the time value of money

**149**   Which ONE of the following does NOT apply to the Modified Rate of Return method?

○   The MIRR measures the economic yield of an investment under the assumption that any cash surpluses are reinvested to earn a return equal to the IRR of the original project.

○   The MIRR gives a measure of the return from the project, whereas the IRR only represents the return from the project if funds can be re-invested at the IRR for the duration of the project.

○   The MIRR gives an indication of the maximum cost of finance that the firm could sustain to allow the project to remain worthwhile.

○   The MIRR overcomes the problem of the reinvestment assumption and the fact that changes in the cost of capital over the life of the project cannot be incorporated in the IRR approach.

**150**   Ontario Ltd's cost of capital is 7% per annum. A project with the following cash flows is under consideration:

| $T_0$ | $T_1$ | $T_2$ | $T_3$ | $T_4$ |
|-------|-------|-------|-------|-------|
| ($22,500) | $7,500 | $7,500 | $7,400 | $7,300 |

The MIRR for the project is closest to:

A     7%

B     8%

C     9%

D     10%

**151**   Michigan Ltd's cost of capital is 9% per annum. A project with the following cash flows is under consideration:

| $T_0$ | $T_1$ | $T_2$ | $T_3$ | $T_4$ |
|-------|-------|-------|-------|-------|
| ($67,000) | $20,000 | $19,500 | $19,000 | $19,000 |

The MIRR for the project is closest to:

A     7%

B     8%

C     9%

D     10%

**152**   Superior Ltd's cost of capital is 6% per annum. A project with the following cash flows is under consideration:

| $T_0$ | $T_1$ | $T_2$ | $T_3$ | $T_4$ |
|-------|-------|-------|-------|-------|
| ($120,000) | $45,000 | $35,000 | $35,000 | $30,000 |

The MIRR for the project is closest to:

A     7%

B     8%

C     9%

D     10%

**153** When compared with the NPV method, the IRR method has a number of disadvantages. What is the validity of the following statements?

(i) The internal rate of return (IRR) ignores the relative size of investments.

(ii) For a project with non-conventional cashflows, the use of the IRR method can prove problematic or misleading.

|   | Statement 1 | Statement 2 |
|---|---|---|
| A | True | True |
| B | True | False |
| C | False | False |
| D | False | True |

**154** The following information relates to a management consultancy:

| | |
|---|---|
| Wage cost per consultant hour (senior consultant) | $45.00 |
| Wage cost per consultant hour (junior consultant) | $26.00 |
| Overhead absorption rate per consultant hour | $20.50 |

The firm adds a 25% mark-up on marginal cost to arrive at the price to charge clients.

For client 'Greenstart' 75 hours of senior consultant time and 30 hours of junior consultant time have been incurred. All staff are paid on an hourly basis.

**What price should be charged to Greenstart? (2 d.p.)**

$ _____

**155** When deciding upon the price of a product, which of the following items would not be taken into consideration?

**Select ALL that apply:**

○ Cost of making the product.

○ Price elasticity of demand.

○ Cost of making other unrelated products.

○ Prices charged by competitors serving the same market segments.

○ Level of customer disposable wealth.

**156** When is market skimming pricing appropriate?

A If demand is very elastic

B If the product is new and different

C If there is little chance of achieving economies of scale

D If demand is inelastic

E If there is little competition and high barriers to entry

157   **Which of the following is a recognised method of arriving at the selling price for the products of a business?**

   (i)     Life cycle pricing

   (ii)    Price skimming

   (iii)   Penetration pricing

   (iv)    Target costing

   A      (i) and (ii) only

   B      (i), (ii) and (iii) only

   C      (ii) and (iii) only

   D      (i), (iii) and (iv) only

   E      (i), (ii), (iii) and (iv)

158   **Which of the following circumstances favour a penetration pricing policy?**

   (i)     There are significant economies of scale from high volume output

   (ii)    Demand is relatively inelastic

   (iii)   The firm wishes to discourage new entrants to the market

   (iv)    The product life cycle is relatively short

   A      (i) and (iii) only

   B      (ii) and (iv) only

   C      (i), (ii) and (iii) only

   D      (ii) and (iii)

   E      (i) and (iv)

159   Maltov has established the following cost and revenue functions for the single product that it manufactures:

   Price = $120 − 0.5 × quantity

   Marginal revenue = $120 − 1 × quantity

   Total cost = $250,000 − 20 × quantity

   **The price should Maltov charge for its product in order to maximise profit is :**

   $ [                    ]

**160** A factory's entire machine capacity is used to produce essential components. The costs of using the machines are as follows:

Variable costs      $15,000

Fixed costs        $50,000

Total              $65,000

**If all the components are purchased from an outside supplier, the machines could be used to produce other items which would earn a total contribution of $25,000. What is the maximum price that a profit- maximising company should be willing to pay to the outside supplier for the components?**

A     $15,000

B     $25,000

C     $40,000

D     $65,000

**161** The trust in charge of national landmarks offers discounted entry to visitors with a valid student identity card.

**This price discrimination policy is on the basis of:**

A     Place

B     Usage

C     Market segment

D     Time

E     Product type

**162** H is launching a new product which it expects to incur a variable cost of $14 per unit. The company has completed some market research to try to determine the optimum selling price with the following results.

If the price charged was to be $25 per unit then the demand would be 1,000 units each period. For every $1 increase in the selling price, demand would reduce by 100 units each period. For every $1 reduction in the selling price, the demand would increase by 100 units each period.

**Calculate:**

**The selling price per unit needed to maximise profit:**

$ [                    ]

**163** Market research by company a has revealed that the maximum demand for product R is 50,000 units each year and that demand will reduce by 50 units for every $1 that the selling price is increased.

Based on this information, company A has calculated that the profit-maximising level of sales for product R for the coming year is 35,000 units.

**The selling price of each of the units at the profit-maximising level of sales is:**

$ [                    ]

**164    SAMSINGING LTD**

'Samsinging Ltd' is about to launch a new product to the UK market, the new product is called the 'Songtime'. Sales demand has been estimated based on product launches in a range of similar countries and the expected demand is to be between a low of 50,000 units per month and a high of 400,000 units per month depending upon the price ultimately charged.

The marketing department believe that 50,000 units would be sold if the price is set at $400 per unit. They have also advised that for every decrease in price of $12.50 per unit, an additional 25,000 units would be sold.

Fixed costs are expected to be $48 million per annum if the company produces 250,000 units or less. However, if the level of production exceeds 250,000 units, annual fixed costs are expected to increase by $6 million.

If 250,000 units or less are made, the variable production cost per unit is expected to be $240 per unit. If more than 250,000 units are made, the variable production cost per unit is expected to be $210 per unit. Variable selling cost per unit is expected to be $35 per unit if 150,000 units or less are sold, and $40 per unit if more than 150,000 units are sold.

Produce a table but consider only production and sales levels of 50,000 units, 100,000 units, 150,000 units, 200,000 units, 250,000 units, 300,000 units, 350,000 units and 400,000 units.

**What price should be set, given that the primary objective is to maximise profit?**

$ 

**165    STALY PLC**

Staly plc has two wholly owned UK-based subsidiaries. One of these subsidiaries, Brompton Ltd, manufactures plastic toys which it sells to toy retailers. Brompton Ltd is about to launch a new product but is unsure what price to charge. A firm of consultants have estimated the level of demand at several different prices. This information is as follows:

| Price ($) | 5 | 10 | 15 | 20 | 25 | 30 | 35 | 40 |
|---|---|---|---|---|---|---|---|---|
| Level of demand in forthcoming year (000 of units) | 200 | 180 | 160 | 135 | 120 | 100 | 75 | 50 |

The cost of manufacturing the new toy has been estimated as follows:

|  | $ per unit |
|---|---|
| Direct materials | 2.00 |
| Direct labour | 1.50 |
| Variable overheads | 2.50 |
|  | 6.00 |

Fixed costs associated with manufacturing the new toy are expected to be $400,000 per annum. However, if production and sales exceed 150,000 units fixed costs are expected to increase by $50,000.

The second subsidiary, Electrics Ltd, assembles desktop computers using components sourced from suppliers of keyboards, microchips, monitors, speakers and so on. It sells these computers under its own brand name through 150 of its own outlets in major shopping centres throughout the UK.

It is to commence selling a new computer aimed at students. The management of Electrics Ltd believe that the price and marginal revenue equations are as follows:

Price equation:

$P = 2,000 - 0.01Q$

where P is selling price and Q is sales quantity in units.

Marginal revenue (MR) equation:

$MR = 2,000 - 0.02Q$

The cost of manufacture is expected to be:

|  | $ per unit |
|---|---|
| Direct materials (bought-in components) | 400 |
| Direct labour (assembly) | 150 |
| Variable overheads | 50 |
| Fixed overheads (apportioned) | 200 |
|  | 800 |

**For Brompton Ltd, what price should be set for the new toy in order to maximise profit?**

$ [                    ]

**What price should be set to maximise profit for Electrics Ltd?**

$ [                    ]

**What price should be set to maximise revenue for Electrics Ltd?**

$ [                    ]

## 166 AVX LTD

AVX plc assembles circuit boards for use by high-technology audio video companies. One particular board is the CB45. Due to the rapidly advancing technology in this field, AVX plc is constantly being challenged to learn new techniques.

AVX plc initially priced each batch of CB45 circuit boards on the basis of its standard cost of $960 plus a mark-up of 25%.

Recently the company has noticed that, due to increasing competition, it is having difficulty maintaining its sales volume at this price.

The Finance Director has agreed that the long-run unit variable cost of the CB45 circuit board is $672.72 per batch. She has suggested that the price charged should be based on an analysis of market demand.

She has discovered that at a price of $1,200 the demand is 16 batches per month, for every $20 reduction in selling price there is an increase in demand of 1 batch of CB45 circuit boards, and for every $20 increase in selling price there is a reduction in demand of 1 batch.

**The profit-maximising selling price per batch using the data supplied by the Finance Director is**

$ [                    ]

**167** Company MtF is reviewing its pricing for one of its products.

The product's marginal costs are $25 per unit and MtF wish to set a price to maximise profits.

**If the product's demand function is P=85 – 0.05X what is the profit maximising price and quantity?**

A    Price = 55 and Quantity = 600

B    Price = 25 and Quantity = 600

C    Price = 45 and Quantity = 1,100

D    Price = 30 and Quantity = 1,100

**168** **Which of the following is NOT a weakness of the economist's pricing model (MC=MR).**

A    It is difficult to identify the demand curve for a product

B    Other factors may affect demand

C    It takes account of the relationship between price and demand

D    A company's strategy may not be to maximise profit in the short term

**169** **From the pricing formula P = a – b X match the element to its correct description.**

| List 1 options | List 2 options |
| --- | --- |
| P | Profit maximising quantity |
| a | Slope of the demand curve |
| b | Profit maximising price |
| X | Intercept on the y axis (price where sales = zero) |

**170** Company TVC is calculating the price of a new product and wishes to use the economists pricing model P= a – bX to reach its profit maximising price.

Market research has determined that for $30 increase in price the demand will fall by 150 units and that maximum demand is 15,000 units.

**The profit maximising quantity is 10,500. The profit maximising price is**

$ _____

**171** **If using the profit maximisation method of pricing when must you use the tabular method?**

A    When b is positive

B    When the demand curve slopes upwards

C    When the relationship between price and demand is not linear

D    When maximum demand is known

## 172   XYZ MOTOR GROUP

XYZ motor group comprises three autonomous divisions and its divisional managers are paid salary bonuses linked to the profit that their respective divisions achieve.

The New Vehicle (NV) division has a city showroom. It sells new vehicles and accepts trade-ins which are sold to the Used Vehicle (UV) division at a 'going trade price' less any necessary repair costs. The Vehicle Repair (VR) division performs necessary repair work to trade-ins and invoices UV for such work on a full cost plus basis. Both the UV and VR divisions do a great deal of business unrelated to trade-ins.

NV has the option of selling a new vehicle to a customer for $40,000 (including a 25% profit mark up on cost) providing the customer is given a trade-in value of $28,000 on his old vehicle. Reference to used car value guides indicate that the going trade price for the trade-in vehicle will be $17,500. However, it is estimated that UV division will be able to sell the trade in for $28,900 after incurring a charge from VR for repairing the vehicle as follows:

|  | $ |
|---|---|
| Variable costs | 500 |
| Fixed overheads | 250 (being 50% of VCs) |
| Mark up | 75 (being 10% on cost) |
| Total | 825 |

**The impact on the contribution of the NV division and XYZ in total of proceeding with the new car sale on the terms specified is**

**The impact on the contribution of the UV division and XYZ in total of proceeding with the new car sale on the terms specified is**

**The impact on the contribution of the VR division and XYZ in total of proceeding with the new car sale on the terms specified is**

**The impact on the contribution of XYZ in total of proceeding with the new car sale on the terms specified is**

# D: MANAGEMENT CONTROL AND RISK

**173** A firm finds that the internal rate of return on a project is 10%, having assumed an inflation rate of 4% on all of its cashflows. If it revises its estimate of inflation to 9%, what would be the revised internal rate of return on the project?

A    9.5%

B    15.3%

C    10.0%

D    13.0%

**174** A local authority is considering automating the purchases system in several departments. Details of the proposed project are as follows:

| | |
|---|---|
| Life of project: | 5 years |
| Initial cost | $75,000 |
| Annual savings: | |
| Labour costs | $20,000 |
| Other costs | $5,000 |
| Cost of capital | 15% per annum |

**The IRR for this project is nearest to:**

A    10.13%

B    14.87%

C    15.64%

D    19.88%

E    20.13%

**175** The percentage change in the annual labour cost savings that could occur before the project ceases to be viable is

A    10.50%

B    11.73%

C    13.13%

D    35.20%

E    44.00%

**176** Company DW is considering a new project which has a projected NPV of $8,800 over an expected life of 5 years.

DW's cost of capital is 10% per annum. Labour cost for the project are $20,000 pa.

**The percentage change in labour cost to two decimal places that could occur before the project becomes unviable is**

A    11.61%

B    44.00%

C    8.80%

D    12.00%

**177** Company FWM has apprised a project with an expected life of six years using NPV and has calculated the project has a negative NPV of $7,500. Few of the costs are controllable however the production director thinks that labour costs could be reduced. Labour currently costs $25,000 pa and FWM's cost of capital is 15%.

**Calculate to two decimal places what percentage the labour costs must be reduced in order to make the project break even:**

**178** **Which of the following is NOT an advantage of sensitivity analysis**

A    It is easy to calculate

B    Identifies critical cash flows

C    Gives management more information for decision making

D    Gives an indication of the likelihood of a variable changing

**179** LFF plc are considering a new project with a five year life span. Due to the unpredictable supply of a key component, the production director has identified three possible levels of variable cost per unit:

| Cost | Probability |
|---|---|
| Optimistic :$30 | 0.3 |
| Likely: $35 | 0.5 |
| Pessimistic:$45 | 0.2 |

Sales of 10,000 pa are expected. LFF PLC use a cost of capital of 12% to appraise projects.

**What is the expected present value of the variable cost to be used in the NPV analysis to the nearest $?**

A    $1,300,000

B    $1,279,775

C    $201,285

D    $355,000

**180** CBG Co is considering a new project with an initial outlay of $80,000. There are several possible market conditions with their associated probabilities.

| | | Year 1 cash | Year 2 cash |
|---|---|---|---|
| Optimistic | 30% | $70,000 | $85,000 |
| Most likely | 45% | $40,000 | $55,000 |
| Pessimistic | 25% | $25,000 | $30,000 |

**CBG Co evaluate their projects using a cost of capital of 10%. To the nearest $, what is the NPV of the project?**

$ [          ]

**181** A company is considering investing in a manufacturing project that would have a three year life span. The investment would involve an immediate cash outflow of $50,000, and have a zero residual value. In each of the three years, 4,000 units would be produced and sold. The contribution per unit, based on current prices, is $5. The company has an annual cost of capital of 8%. It is expected that the inflation rate will be 3% in each of the next three years.

**The net present value of the project (to the nearest $500) is:**

A    $4,500

B    $5,000

C    $5,500

D    $6,000

E    $6,500

**182** A company is considering investing in a manufacturing project that would have a three year life span. The investment would involve an immediate cash outflow of $50,000, and have a zero residual value. In each of the three years, 4,000 units would be produced and sold. The contribution per unit, based on current prices, is $5. The company has an annual cost of capital of 8%. It is expected that the inflation rate will be 3% in each of the next three years.

**If the annual inflation rate is now projected to be 4%, the maximum monetary cost of capital for this project to remain viable is (to the nearest 0.5%)**

A    13.0%

B    13.5%

C    14.0%

D    14.5%

E    15.0%

**183** A company is evaluating a new product proposal. The proposed product selling price is $220 per unit and the variable costs are $55 per unit. The incremental cash fixed costs for the product will be $190,000 per annum. The discounted cash flow calculations results in a positive NPV:

|  |  | Cash flow | Discount rate | Present value |
|---|---|---|---|---|
|  |  | $ |  | $ |
| Year 0 | Initial outlay | (2,000,000) | 1.000 | (2,000,000) |
| Year 1–6 | Annual cash flow | 450,000 | 4.623 | 2,080,350 |
| Year 6 | Sale of assets | 75,000 | 0.630 | 47,250 |
| Net present value |  |  |  | 127,600 |

**What is the percentage change in selling price that would result in the project having a net present value of zero?**

A    3.2%

B    4.6%

C    5.9%

D    7.0%

**184** A company is carrying out sensitivity analysis on an investment project. The initial DCF analysis, at a cost of capital of 10%, is as follows:

| Year | Item | Cash flow | Discount factor at 10% | PV |
|---|---|---|---|---|
|  |  | $ |  | $ |
| 0 | Cost of machine | (50,000) | 1.000 | (50,000) |
| 1 | Net cash flow from sales | 22,000 | 0.909 | 19,998 |
| 2 | Net cash flow from sales | 22,000 | 0.826 | 18,172 |
| 3 | Net cash flow from sales | 10,000 | 0.751 | 7,510 |
| 3 | Residual value of the machine | 10,000 | 0.751 | 7,510 |
| NPV |  |  |  | + 3,190 |

The investment is in a machine that will make a product, Product Q. Product Q will sell for $40 per unit, and will have a variable cost of $10 per unit. Annual sales will be 1,000 units in years 1 and 2, and 600 units in year 3. Additional fixed cost expenditure on cash items will be $8,000 each year.

The residual value of the machine will be 20% of the initial cost of the machine.

**To the nearest 0.1%, by how much could the selling price per unit of the product fall short of the expected $40 without the project ceasing to be viable, given no change in any of the other cash flow estimates?**

A    3.6%

B    6.0%

C    6.1%

D    7.0%

**185** A company is carrying out sensitivity analysis on an investment project. The initial DCF analysis, at a cost of capital of 10%, is as follows:

| Year | Item | Cash flow | Discount factor at 10% | PV |
|---|---|---|---|---|
| | | $ | | $ |
| 0 | Cost of machine | (50,000) | 1.000 | (50,000) |
| 1 | Net cash flow from sales | 22,000 | 0.909 | 19,998 |
| 2 | Net cash flow from sales | 22,000 | 0.826 | 18,172 |
| 3 | Net cash flow from sales | 10,000 | 0.751 | 7,510 |
| 3 | Residual value of the machine | 10,000 | 0.751 | 7,510 |
| NPV | | | | + 3,190 |

The investment is in a machine that will make a product, Product Q. Product Q will sell for $40 per unit, and will have a variable cost of $10 per unit. Annual sales will be 1,000 units in years 1 and 2, and 600 units in year 3. Additional fixed cost expenditure on cash items will be $8,000 each year.

The residual value of the machine will be 20% of the initial cost of the machine.

**To the nearest $1,000, what is the maximum amount that the machine can cost, without the project ceasing to be viable, given no change in any of the other cash flow estimates?**

A    $53,000

B    $54,000

C    $55,000

D    $56,000

**186** A project has a net present value of $320,000.

The sales revenues for the project have a total pre-discounted value of $900,000 and a total present value of $630,000 after tax.

**The sensitivity of the investment to changes in the value of sales is closest to:**

A    $310,000

B    $580,000

C    51%

D    36%

**187** An education authority is considering the implementation of a CCTV (closed circuit television) security system in one of its schools.

Details of the proposed project are as follows:

| | |
|---|---|
| Life of project | 5 years |
| Initial cost | $75,000 |

*Annual savings:*

| | |
|---|---|
| Labour costs | $20,000 |
| Other costs | $5,000 |

Cost of capital     15% per annum

**Calculate:**

**The internal rate of return for this project:**

[            ] %

**The percentage change in the annual labour cost savings that could occur before the project ceased to be viable:**

[            ] %

**188** The management accountant of Bar Company has estimated that the cash flows for Project X would be as follows:

| Year | Investment | Running costs | Savings |
|---|---|---|---|
| | $ | $ | $ |
| 0 | (120,000) | | |
| 1 | | (80,000) | 150,000 |
| 2 | | (100,000) | 160,000 |
| 3 | | (120,000) | 170,000 |
| 4 | | (150,000) | 180,000 |

The project has a positive NPV of $22,900 when discounted at the company's cost of capital, which is 20% per annum.

On reviewing the cost estimates, the management accountant decides that the running costs will in fact be 20% higher each year than originally estimated, although savings will be higher too.

**Calculate the minimum percentage that annual savings must be higher than originally estimated for the project to remain viable.**

[            ] %

**189** Shuffles is attempting to decide which size of fork-lift truck to buy in its warehouses. There are three grades of truck, the A series, B series and the C series. The uncertainty faced is the expected growth in the on-line market it serves, which could grow at 15%, 30% or even 40% in the next period.

Shuffles Limited has correctly produced the following decision table and has calculated the average daily contribution gained from each combination of truck and growth assumption.

| Decision table | | | Type of truck | | |
|---|---|---|---|---|---|
| | | | A series | B series | C series |
| Growth rate | | 15% | $2,400 | $1,800 | $3,600 |
| | | 30% | $1,400 | $1,900 | $4,500 |
| | | 40% | $4,900 | $2,800 | $3,900 |

**Which truck would the pessimistic buyer get?**

**Which truck would the optimistic buyer get?**

. **If the buyer were prone to regretting decisions that have been made which truck would he get?**

**If the probabilities of the given growth rates are**

**15%: 0.4, 30%: 0.25 and 40%: 0.35, which truck would the risk neutral buyer get?**

**190** The following statements have been made about the use of simulation.

**Select ALL that apply:**

- ○ Simulation models the behaviour of a system.
- ○ Simulation models can be used to study alternative solutions to a problem.
- ○ The equations describing the operating characteristics of the system are known.
- ○ A simulation model cannot prescribe what should be done about a problem.

**191** A company can make either of two new products, X and Y, but not both. The profitability of each product depends on the state of the market, as follows:

| Market state | Profit from product | | Probability of market state |
|---|---|---|---|
| | X $ | Y $ | |
| Good | 20,000 | 17,000 | 0.2 |
| Fair | 15,000 | 16,000 | 0.5 |
| Poor | 6,000 | 7,000 | 0.3 |

**What is the expected value of perfect information as to the state of the market?**

A    $0

B    $600

C    $800

D    $1,000

**192** A company is considering the development and marketing of a new product. Development costs will be $2m. There is a 75% probability that the development effort will be successful, and a 25% probability that it will be unsuccessful. If development is successful and the product is marketed, it is estimated that:

| | Expected profit | Probability |
|---|---|---|
| Product very successful | $6.0m | 0.4 |
| Product moderately successful | $1.8m | 0.4 |
| Product unsuccessful | ($5.0m) | 0.2 |

**What is the expected value of the project?**

A    ($0.41m)

B    $2.12m

C    $1.59m

D    $0.12m

**193** Dough Distributors has decided to increase its daily muffin purchases by 100 boxes. A box of muffins costs $2 and sells for $3 through regular stores. Any boxes not sold through regular stores are sold through Dough's thrift store for $1. Dough assigns the following probabilities to selling additional boxes:

| Additional sales | Probability |
|---|---|
| 60 boxes | 60% |
| 100 boxes | 40% |

**What is the expected value of Dough's decision to buy 100 additional boxes of muffins?**

A    $52

B    $68

C    $28

D    $40

**194** To assist in an investment decision, Gift Co. selected the most likely sales volume from several possible outcomes. Which of the following attributes would that selected sales volume reflect?

A     The greatest probability

B     The expected value

C     The mid-point of the range

D     The median

**195** Your client wants your advice on which of two alternatives he should choose. One alternative is to sell an investment now for $10,000. An alternative is to hold the investment three days after which he can sell it for a certain selling price based on the following probabilities:

| Selling price | Probability |
|---|---|
| $5,000 | 40% |
| $8,000 | 20% |
| $12,000 | 30% |
| $30,000 | 10% |

**Using probability theory, which of the following is the most reasonable statement?**

A     Hold the investment three days because the expected value of holding exceeds the current selling price.

B     Hold the investment three days because of the chance of getting $30,000 for it.

C     Sell the investment now because the current selling price exceeds the expected value of holding.

D     Sell the investment now because there is a 60% chance that the selling price will fall in three days.

**196** Leslie Company is an intermediary supplier of parts to several manufacturing companies. As the accounting consultant for Leslie Company you have compiled data on the day-to-day demand rate from Leslie's customers for Product A and the lead time to receive Product A from its supplier. The data are summarized in the following probability tables:

Demand for Product A

| Unit demand per day | Probability of occurrence |
|---|---|
| 0 | 45% |
| 1 | 15% |
| 2 | 30% |
| 3 | 10% |

Lead time for Product A

| Lead time in days | Probability of occurrence |
|---|---|
| 1 | 40% |
| 2 | 35% |
| 3 | 25% |

Leslie is able to deliver Product A to its customers the same day that Product A is received from its supplier. All units of Product A demanded but not available, due to a stock-out, are backordered and are filled immediately when a new shipment arrives.

**The probability of the demand for Product A being nine units during a 3-day lead time for delivery from the supplier is:**

A  0.00025

B  0.10

C  0.025

D  0.25

**197** A company knows that sales for a new product will either be at a high level, or at a low level. There is a 65% chance that sales will be at a high level. A market research company will predict the future sales level. Their forecasts are known to be correct 85% of the time.

**If the company receives a forecast of low sales from the market researchers, what is the probability that they will subsequently achieve high sales?**

A  75.32%

B  9.75%

C  39.5%

D  29.75%

E  24.68%

**198** 30% of the new cakes of a particular recipe are supplied from bakery A, the other 70% from bakery B. 10% of the cakes from Bakery A are not baked properly (they decompose when they are taken out of their box). 12% of the cakes from Bakery B are not baked properly either.

**Mr M has just bought a new cake, which is not baked properly. What is the probability that that cake was made in Bakery B? (2 d.p.)**

**199  RECYC**

Recyc plc is a company which reprocesses factory waste in order to extract good quality aluminium. Information concerning its operations is as follows:

(1)  Recyc plc places an advance order each year for chemical X for use in the aluminium extraction process. It will enter into an advance contract for the coming year for chemical X at one of three levels – high, medium or low, which correspond to the requirements of a high, medium or low level of waste available for reprocessing.

(2)  The level of waste available will not be known when the advance order for chemical X is entered into. A set of probabilities have been estimated by management as to the likelihood of the quantity of waste being at a high, medium or low level.

(3)  Where the advance order entered into for chemical X is lower than that required for the level of waste for processing actually received, a discount from the original demand price is allowed by the supplier for the total quantity of chemical X actually required.

(4)  Where the advance order entered into for chemical X is in excess of that required to satisfy the actual level of waste for reprocessing, a penalty payment in excess of the original demand price is payable for the total quantity of chemical X actually required.

A summary of the information relating to the above points is as follows:

| | | | Chemical X costs per kg | | |
|---|---|---|---|---|---|
| Level of reprocessing | Waste available 000 kg | Probability | Advance order $ | Conversion discount $ | Conversion premium $ |
| High | 50,000 | 0.30 | 1.00 | | |
| Medium | 38,000 | 0.50 | 1.20 | | |
| Low | 30,000 | 0.20 | 1.40 | | |
| Chemical X:  order conversion: | | | | | |
|    Low to medium | | | | 0.10 | |
|    Medium to high | | | | 0.10 | |
|    Low to high | | | | 0.15 | |
|    Medium to low | | | | | 0.25 |
|    High to medium | | | | | 0.25 |
|    High to low | | | | | 0.60 |

Aluminium is sold at $0.65 per kg. Variable costs (excluding chemical X costs) are 70% of sales revenue. Aluminium extracted from the waste is 15% of the waste input. Chemical X is added to the reprocessing at the rate of 1 kg per 100 kg of waste.

Complete a summary which shows the budgeted contribution earned by Recyc plc for the coming year for each of nine possible outcomes:

|  |  | Level of waste | | |
|---|---|---|---|---|
|  |  | High | Medium | Low |
| Advance order of chemical | High |  |  |  |
|  | Medium |  |  |  |
|  | Low |  |  |  |

State the contribution for the coming year which corresponds to the use of:

(i) maximax

$ [                    ]

and (ii) maximin decision criteria.

$ [                    ]

## 200 TICKET AGENT

A ticket agent has an arrangement with a concert hall that holds concerts on 60 nights a year whereby he receives discounts as follows per concert:

| For purchase of: | He receives a discount of: |
|---|---|
| 200 tickets | 20% |
| 300 tickets | 25% |
| 400 tickets | 30% |
| 500 tickets or more | 40% |

Purchases must be in full hundreds. The average price per ticket is $30.

He must decide in advance each year the number of tickets he will purchase. If he has any tickets unsold by the afternoon of the concert he must return them to the box office. If the box office sells any of these he receives 60% of their price.

His sales records over a few years show that for a concert with extremely popular artistes he can be confident of selling 500 tickets, for one with lesser known artistes 350 tickets, and for one with relatively unknown artistes 200 tickets.

His records show that 10% of the tickets he returns are sold by the box office. (**Note:** these are in addition to any sales made by the ticket agent).

His administration costs incurred in selling tickets are the same per concert irrespective of the popularity of the artistes.

Sales records show that the frequency of concerts will be:

| With popular artistes | 45% |
|---|---|
| With lesser known artistes | 30% |
| With unknown artistes | 25% |
|  | ——— |
|  | 100% |
|  | ——— |

**Calculate the expected demand for tickets per concert:**

**Calculate the level of his purchases of tickets per concert that will give him the largest profit over a long period of time:**

**Calculate the profit per concert that this level of purchases of tickets will yield:**

$

**Calculate the number of tickets the agent should buy, based on the following criteria:**

Maximin

Maximax

Minimax regret

## 201   SHIFTERS HAULAGE

Shifters Haulage (SH) is considering changing some of the vans it uses to transport crates for customers. The new vans come in three sizes; small, medium and large. SH is unsure about which type to buy. The capacity is 100 crates for the small van, 150 for the medium van and 200 for the large van. Demand for crates varies and can be either 120 or 190 crates per period, with the probability of the higher demand figure being 0.6.

The sale price per crate is $10 and the variable cost $4 per crate for all van sizes subject to the fact that if the capacity of the van is greater than the demand for crates in a period then the variable cost will be lower by 10% to allow for the fact that the vans will be partly empty when transporting crates.

SH is concerned that if the demand for crates exceeds the capacity of the vans then customers will have to be turned away. SH estimates that in this case goodwill of $100 would be charged against profits per period to allow for lost future sales regardless of the number of customers that are turned away.

Depreciation charged would be $200 per period for the small, $300 for the medium and $400 for the large van.

SH has in the past been very aggressive in its decision-making, pressing ahead with rapid growth strategies. However, its managers have recently grown more cautious as the business has become more competitive.

Complete a profits table showing the SIX possible profit figures per period.

### 202   COOL SYSTEMS

Cool Systems, a producer of air conditioning systems for customers in the building trade, is having some problems with the manufacturing process for a particular system, the Breeze. Under its current production process, 25% of the Breeze units are defective. The unit contribution of this system is $40 per unit. Under contract the company has with its customers, Cool systems refunds $60 for each 'Breeze' that the customer finds to be defective; the customers then repair the system to make it usable in their building work.

Before delivering the systems to customers, Cool Systems could spend an additional $30 per Breeze to rework any systems thought to be defective – regardless of whether the system really is defective. The reworked systems can be sold at the regular price and will definitely not be defective in the builders' projects. Unfortunately, Cool Systems cannot tell ahead of time which systems will fail to work in their builders' installations, but would not deliver a system where tests had revealed a problem.

The summary table that shows the budgeted contribution per unit earned by Cool Systems for each of the possible 4 outcomes has been correctly prepared as follows:

|  | Breeze system is not defective | Breeze system is defective |
|---|---|---|
| Cool Systems chooses to rework | $40 – $30 = $10 | $40 – $30 = $10 |
| Cool Systems chooses NOT to rework | $40 | $40 – $60 = ($20) |

A consultant engineer has developed a simple test device to evaluate the system before delivering. For each system, the test device registers positive (i.e. no problem), inconclusive or negative. The test is not perfect, but it is consistent for a particular system; this means the test yields the same result for a given system regardless of how many times it is tested.

To calibrate the test device, it was run on a sample batch of 100 systems. The results are presented in the table below:

|  | System in good condition: 75 systems in total | System in defective condition: 25 systems in total |
|---|---|---|
| Test result : Positive | 52.5 systems | 2.5 systems |
| Test result : Inconclusive | 15 systems | 7.5 systems |
| Test result : Negative | 7.5 systems | 15 systems |

**What is the maximum (per system) the company should be willing to pay for using the test device? Use a decision tree approach to calculate your answer.**

$ [                    ]

## 203 THEATRE

A theatre has a seating capacity of 500 people and is considering engaging MS and her orchestra for a concert for one night only. The fee that would be charged by MS would be $10,000. If the theatre engages MS, then this sum is payable regardless of the size of the theatre audience.

Based on past experience of events of this type, the price of the theatre ticket would be $25 per person. The size of the audience for this event is uncertain, but based on past experience it is expected to be as follows:

|  | *Probability* |
|---|---|
| 300 people | 50% |
| 400 people | 30% |
| 500 people | 20% |

In addition to the sale of the theatre tickets, it can be expected that members of the audience will also purchase confectionery both prior to the performance and during the interval. The contribution that this would yield to the theatre is unclear, but has been estimated as follows:

| *Contribution from confectionery sales* | *Probability* |
|---|---|
| Contribution of $3 per person | 30% |
| Contribution of $5 per person | 50% |
| Contribution of $10 per person | 20% |

**What is the expected value of profits if MS is engaged for the concert?**

$ [                    ]

**Prepare a two-way data table to show the profit values that could occur from deciding to engage MS for the concert:**

| *Confectionary sales* | *$3 per person* | *$5 per person* | *$10 per person* |
|---|---|---|---|
| *Ticket sales* | | | |
| 300 people | | | |
| 400 people | | | |
| 500 people | | | |

## 204  AMELIE

Amelie is setting up in business importing French cheeses. She could open up a small shop, a large outlet, or no shop at all if she decides to sell online only (which she won't be able to do for another few years at least.)

There will be a 5 year lease on a few shops currently available in the centre of town, and Amelie wants to make the correct decision.

Amelie is also thinking about hiring a consultant to conduct a market research study. If the study is conducted, the results could indicate that the cheese market is either favourable or unfavourable.

Amelie believes there is a 50-50 chance that the market will be favourable, and expects her profits to be as follows if she opens her shop:

|  | Favourable market | Unfavourable market |
|---|---|---|
| Large shop | $60,000 | ($40,000) loss |
| Small shop | $30,000 | ($10,000) loss |

The consultant has quoted a charge of $5,000 for the marketing research. He has also hinted that there is a 0.6 probability that the survey will indicate that the cheese market would be favourable.

There is a 0.9 probability that the cheese market will be favourable given a favourable outcome from the study.

The consultant warned Amelie that there is only a probability of 0.12 of a favourable market if the marketing research results are not favourable. Amelie is confused.

A decision tree for Amelie has correctly been drawn as follows to explain whether Amelie should hire the market research consultant:

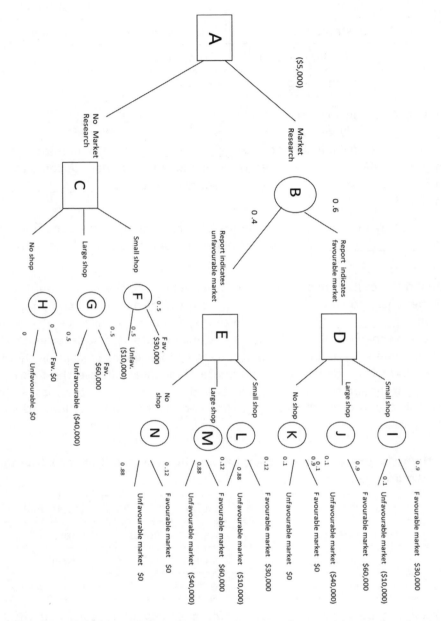

After discussing the competence of the consultant with another business owner, Amelie now believes that she'd rather contact another market research company which guarantees perfect information concerning the cheese market profitability.

**Calculate the value of this perfect information.**

205   **Which concept is not part of the 3V's of Big Data?**

   A   Volume

   B   Variety

   C   Valorisation

   D   Velocity

**206** Complete the following text by selecting the missing words and phrases (the same word may be used more than once):

| external | gather | analyse | traditional |
|---|---|---|---|
| websites | unstructured | Social networks | planning |
| insights | customer demands | structured | systems |
| | customer experience | features | |

Big Data management involves using sophisticated _____ to _____, store and _____ large volumes of data in a variety of _____ and _____ formats. In addition to _____ data from internal sources such as sales history, preferences, order frequency and pricing information, companies can also gather information from _____ sources such as _____, trade publications and _____.

Collating and analysing these large volumes of information allows companies to gain a variety of _____ into customer behaviour and this can help to more accurately predict _____.

These demand forecasts may be in terms of volume but also the type of products required and this is beneficial to company _____ but can also help the company to improve aspects of the _____. In terms of volume predictions, these can help to ensure that a company will always have sufficient inventory to satisfy demand. This will mean that customers do not need to wait to receive their goods which is likely to be a key part of their shopping experience. Furthermore companies can use the information and _____ to understand which products and _____ are most popular with customers. This can inform product re-design to ensure that any revisions are in line with customer preferences.

**207** Complete the following text by selecting the missing words and phrases (the same word may be used more than once):

| volume | storage | useful | traditional |
|---|---|---|---|
| websites | data | Social networks | sources |
| insights | wasted | variety | systems |
| standard | velocity | features | e-commerce |

Business data can be difficult to manage for a variety of reasons and these can be summarised using the 3 V's of velocity, volume and variety.

- The first 'V is '_____': the speed at which data is now generated from sources such as social media networks makes it incredibly difficult for _____ database management systems to cope and give relevant and timely _____. If this_____ is not managed effectively it is, at best, _____ but could also result in significant increases in the data _____ capacity required, without seeing any particular benefits.

- The second 'V is '_____ ': Companies can now gather and generate data from a huge range of _____including internal systems, _____ sources, competitor and customer websites and social media networks. Not only has the overall _____ of sources increased but the amount of data gathered from each source is now much higher than from _____ reporting. For example the data gathered from a single e-commerce sales transaction can be up to ten times higher than a _____ in-store transaction. It is important that data is only gathered (and therefore stored and analysed) from relevant _____ that can actually add value to company decision making as there is a danger that companies become obsessed with gathering all data that is available rather than just that which is _____.

- The third 'V is '_____ ': An increasing number of incompatible and inconsistent data formats is emerging at a fast rate. Most traditional data management _____ are based around extracting data from, and storing data in, standard formats such as XML. Collecting data in a wide variety of formats including sound files and GPS data creates challenges for a system managing such big data.

208 A business is faced with a risk that has a low probability of occurring and a high negative impact if it does occur, but the related activity cannot be avoided because it is strategically vital to undertake for the business.

**Which of the following strategies is likely to be best suited to dealing with this risk?**

A    Transfer

B    Avoid

C    Reduce

D    Accept

209 A business is faced with a risk that has a high probability of occurring and a high negative impact if it does occur. It is not strategically vital for the business to undertake the activity.

**Which of the following strategies is likely to be best suited to dealing with this risk?**

A    Transfer

B    Avoid

C    Reduce

D    Accept

210 A business is faced with a risk that has a low probability of occurring and a low negative impact if it does occur. The risk is not really a matter, even if it is realised.

**Which of the following strategies is likely to be best suited to dealing with this risk?**

A    Transfer

B    Avoid

C    Reduce

D    Accept

**211** A business is faced with a risk that has a high probability of occurring and a low negative impact if it does occur. The business is thinking about using a different method to carry out the activity.

**Which of the following strategies is likely to be best suited to dealing with this risk?**

A     Transfer

B     Avoid

C     Reduce

D     Accept

**212** **In a group of 100 CIMA students, 30 are male, 55 are studying for Certificate Stage and 6 of the male students are not studying for Certificate Stage. A student chosen at random is female. What is the probability that she is not studying Certificate Stage?**

A     0.80

B     0.56

C     0.44

D     0.20

**213** Mail order buyers of Brand X classified by area and age (years)

| Age | Under 25 | 25–44 | 45–64 | 65 + |
|---|---|---|---|---|
| *Area* | | | | |
| North | 400 | 350 | 300 | 250 |
| South | 600 | 550 | 500 | 450 |
| East | 200 | 150 | 100 | 50 |
| West | 400 | 350 | 300 | 250 |
| Totals | 1,600 | 1,400 | 1,200 | 1,000 |

**Calculate:**

The probability that a randomly-selected brand x buyer is from the north and under 25 years of age is (to 2 decimal places):

P = [                    ]

The probability that a randomly-selected Brand X buyer is from the West or under 25 years of age is (to 2 decimal places):

P = [                    ]

The probability that a randomly-selected Brand X buyer, who is under 25 years of age, is from the South is (to 3 decimal places):

P = [                    ]

The probability that two randomly-selected Brand X buyers are both under 25 years of age is (to two decimal places):

P = [                    ]

# Section 2

# ANSWERS TO OBJECTIVE TEST QUESTIONS

## A: COST PLANNING AND ANALYSIS FOR COMPETITIVE ADVANTAGE

**1      B**

|  | E | F | G | Total |
|---|---|---|---|---|
| Budgeted number of batches to be produced: | 75,000/200 = 375 | 120,000/60 = 2,000 | 60,000/30 = 2,000 | |
| Machine set-ups per batch: | 5 | 3 | 9 | |
| Total machine set-ups | 1,875 | 6,000 | 18,000 | 25,875 |

So budgeted cost per set-up: $180,000/25,875 = $6.96 per set-up

Therefore the budgeted machine set-up cost per unit of F produced is:

($6.96 × 3)/60 = $0.35 per unit or $6.96 × 6,000/120,000 = $0.35 per unit

**2      A**

Since all of the activities listed are directly related to the goods that are sold in the supermarket, DPP (based on ABC) requires that all of the costs should be included in the calculation.

**3      B**

Pareto analysis is a cumulative analysis, taking the items in descending order of size. Here, the products should be in descending order of total sales revenue earned.

| Product | Sales revenue |
|---|---|
| | $ |
| D | 100,000 |
| A | 50,000 |
| B | 40,000 |
| C | 30,000 |
| E | 20,000 |

240,000

**4** (i) Set ups

1 for every 10 units of A, 1 for every 10 units of B, 1 per day for C = 50 + 40 + 20 = 110
Charge out rate = \$2,200/110 = \$20 per driver

Total charge to C = 20 × \$20 = \$400

Cost per unit for Gamma = \$400/20 = \$20

(ii) Inspections

Ratio is 1:1:2 = 500 + 400 + 40 = 940

Charge out rate = \$2,820/940 = \$3 per driver

Total charge to Gamma = 40 × \$3 = \$120

Cost per unit for Gamma = \$120/20 = \$6

So total cost per unit for Gamma = \$26.00

**5** **B**

**6** All statements apply.

First, the results are rearranged in descending order of contribution and a cumulative contribution figure calculated.

| Product | Contribution | Cumulative contribution | Cumulative |
|---|---|---|---|
| | $(000) | $(000) | % |
| White loaves | 94 | 94 | 25 |
| Individual cakes | 83 | 177 | 46 |
| Brown loaves | 67 | 244 | 64 |
| Family-sized cakes | 53 | 297 | 78 |
| Plain rolls | 42 | 339 | 89 |
| Filled rolls | 26 | 365 | 96 |
| Pasties and pies | 16 | 381 | 100 |
| | 381 | | |

The cumulative data can now be used to produce the required Pareto chart showing product contribution:

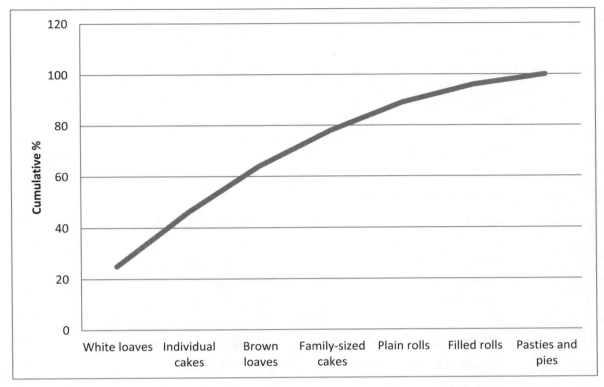

It is clear from the diagram that four of the product lines make up nearly 80% of the contribution for the bakery firm.

The most popular products are bread and cakes and with white loaves outselling all other products. Management attention should be focused on these areas.

**7** A cost driver is any factor that causes a change in the cost of an activity, so the most important factor when selecting a cost driver is to identify a *causal* relationship between the cost driver and the costs. Such a relationship may arise because of some physical relationship or because of the logic of the situation.

For example, quality inspection costs are caused by the action of carrying out an inspection to ensure quality standards are being achieved, so the appropriate cost driver would be the number of inspections carried out. Some activities may have multiple cost drivers associated with them; in such a situation it is best if the costs can be analysed into separate cost pools for each of which a single driver can be identified.

**8**

| | | |
|---|---|---|
| Power: | $12,575 | per KJ |
| Stores: | $3,776 | per order |
| Maintenance: | $2,246 | per machine hour |
| Machinery cleaning: | $2,439 | per set-up |

The budgeted costs are:

| Activity | Total $000 | Appropriate cost driver |
|---|---|---|
| Power | 1,250 | Power (kj) per batch |
| Stores | 1,850 | Purchase orders per batch |
| Maintenance | 2,100 | Machine hours per batch |
| Machinery cleaning | 800 | Machine set-ups per batch |
| Indirect labour | 1,460 | Standard labour hours per batch |

For each activity we must calculate a cost driver rate.

**Power**

Total budgeted power $= (1.4 \times 36) + (1.7 \times 10) + (0.8 \times 40)$

$= 99.4$ kj

$\therefore$ Cost driver rate $= \dfrac{\$1.25m}{99.4} = \$12,575$ per kj

**Stores**

Total budgeted purchase orders $= (5 \times 36) + (3 \times 10) + (7 \times 40)$

$= 490$ orders

$\therefore$ Cost driver rate $= \dfrac{\$1.85m}{490} = \$3,776$ per order

**Maintenance**

Total budgeted machine hours $= (10 \times 36) + (7.5 \times 10) + (12.5 \times 40) = 935$ hours

$\therefore$ Cost driver rate $= \dfrac{\$2.1m}{935} = \$2,246$ per machine hour

**Machinery cleaning**

Total budgeted machine set-ups $(3 \times 36) + (2 \times 10) + (5 \times 40)$

$= 328$ set-ups

$\therefore$ Cost driver rate $= \dfrac{\$0.8m}{328} = \$2,439$ per set-up

**9**     Overheads absorbed on machine hour basis

Machine hour absorption rate = Total overheads/Total machine hours

$$= \frac{\$10,430+\$5,250+\$3,600+\$2,100+\$4,620}{(120\times4)+(100\times3)+(80\times2)+(120\times3)} = \frac{\$26,000}{1,300} = \$20 \text{ per machine hour}$$

|  | Total costs in $ |
|---|---|
| Product A | $17,760 |
| Product B | $13,100 |
| Product C | $6,720 |
| Product D | $16,920 |

**Workings – Total costs based on machine hour basis**

|  | A | B | C | D |
|---|---|---|---|---|
|  | $ | $ | $ | $ |
| Direct materials | 40 | 50 | 30 | 60 |
| Direct labour | 28 | 21 | 14 | 21 |
| Production overhead | 80 | 60 | 40 | 60 |
| Production cost/unit | 148 | 131 | 841 | 141 |
| Output in units | 120 | 100 | 80 | 120 |
| Total production cost | $17,760 | $13,100 | $6,720 | $16,920 |

Overheads absorbed based on ABC

|  |  | Total costs in $ |
|---|---|---|
| **Product A** |  | $16,331 |
| **Product B** |  | $13,257 |
| **Product C** | $7,984 |  |
| **Product D** | $16,928 |  |

|  |  | Overhead costs |  |
|---|---|---|---|
|  | $ | Level of activity | Cost/activity |
| Machine department cost | 10,430 | 1,300 | $8.02/hour |
| Set-up costs | 5,250 | 21* | $250.00/run |
| Stores receiving costs | 3,600 | 80** | $45.00/requisition |
| Inspection/quality costs | 2,100 | 21* | $100.00/run |
| Material handling and despatch | 4,620 | 42 | $110.00/order |

**Workings**

\* No of production runs     = output in units/20

$$= \frac{120+100+80+120}{20}$$

$$= \frac{420}{20} = 21$$

\*\*No of requisition raised     = No. of products × 20

    = 4 × 20 = 80

**Total costs based on ABC**

| | A | B | C | D |
|---|---|---|---|---|
| | $ | $ | $ | $ |
| Direct materials | 40.00 | 50.00 | 30.00 | 60.00 |
| Direct labour | 28.00 | 21.00 | 14.00 | 21.00 |
| Machine dept costs | 32.09 | 24.07 | 16.05 | 24.07 |
| Set-up costs | 12.50 | 12.50 | 12.50 | 12.50 |
| Stores receiving | 7.50 | 9.00 | 11.25 | 7.50 |
| Inspection | 5.00 | 5.00 | 5.00 | 5.00 |
| Material handling | 011.00 | 011.00 | 011.00 | 011.00 |
| Production cost/unit | 136.09 | 132.57 | 99.80 | 141.07 |
| Output in units | 00120 | 00100 | 0080 | 00120 |
| Total production costs | $16,331 | $13,257 | $7,984 | $16,928 |

**10    B**

| Average time for first | 1 unit | = | 7 hours |
|---|---|---|---|
| Average time for first | 2 units | = | $0.9 \times 7 = 6.3$ hours |
| Average time for first | 4 units | = | $0.9^2 \times 7 = 5.67$ hours |
| Average time for first | 8 units | = | $0.9^3 \times 7 = 5.103$ hours |

| | | *Hours* |
|---|---|---|
| Total time for first 4 units = | $4 \times 5.67 =$ | 22.680 |
| Total time for first 8 units = | $8 \times 5.103 =$ | 40.824 |
| $\therefore$ Total time for units 5 to 8 = | | 18.144 |

**11**    As output doubles, cumulative time per unit reduces by 75%.

| Units | Average time/unit (minutes) | Total time (minutes) |
|---|---|---|
| 1 | 12.00 | 12.00 |
| 2 | $12.00 \times 75\% = 9.00$ | $9.00 \times 2 = 18.00$ |
| 4 | $9.00 \times 75\% = 6.75$ | $6.75 \times 4 = 27.00$ |

Total time = 27 minutes

**12**

| Units | Cumulative average time | Total time |
|---|---|---|
| 1 | 3 | 3 |
| 2 | | |
| 4 | 2.091675 | 8.3667 |

The learning curve model states that the cumulative average time taken falls by the learning rate each time output doubles. Therefore:

$3 \times r \times r = 2.091675$

$r^2 = 2.091675/3 = 0.835$

The learning rate is 83.5%

**13**

|  | Cumulative average time | | Total time |
|---|---|---|---|
| For first 7 units y = $6 \times 7^{-0.415}$ = | 2.676 | $\times 7$ = | 18.72982 |
| For first 6 units y = $6 \times 6^{-0.415}$ = | 2.8525 | $\times 6$ = | 17.11472 |
| Time for 7th assignment | | | 1.6151 |

Answer 1.62 hours to nearest 0.01 hours

**Key answer tips**

Do not round your workings too early as this will introduce an error. It is preferable to leave full figures in your calculator as far as possible when carrying out the workings.

**14    B**

Time taken for 5 units:

| Y | = | $ax^{-b}$ |
|---|---|---|
| Y | = | $21 \times 5^{-0.3219}$ |
|  | = | $21 \times 0.595664277$ |
|  | = | 12.52 minutes |

Time taken for 6 units:

| Y | = | $ax^{-b}$ |
|---|---|---|
| Y | = | $21 \times 6^{-0.3219}$ |
|  | = | $21 \times 0.561711237$ |
|  | = | 11.80 minutes |

|  | Minutes |
|---|---|
| Total time taken for 6 units at 11.80 minutes = | 70.80 |
| Total time taken for 5 units at 12.51 minutes = | 62.55 |
| Therefore time taken for 6th unit | 8.25 |

**15    C**

External failure costs are those incurred due to poor quality of goods delivered to customers; therefore this includes compensation costs.

Appraisal costs are those incurred in the measuring of quality of output; therefore this includes test equipment running costs.

**16    B**

Machine cells, multi-skilled labour and a close relationship with suppliers are all features of JIT. A focus on inventory being held at a bottleneck resource is a feature of throughput accounting.

**17 D**

Statements A, B and C are incorrect. JIT makes an organisation more vulnerable to disruptions in the supply chain because there are no buffer inventories as protection against a breakdown in supply. JIT is easier to implement when an organisation operates within a narrow geographical area, and close to its suppliers. (At Toyota, where JIT originated, manufacturing operations were initially carried out within a 50 kilometre radius.) With little or no inventories, the risk of inventory obsolescence should not exist.

Statement D is correct. When demand is difficult to predict, it becomes more difficult to operate a demand-driven operation.

**18 B**

(i) is true. JIT is a 'pull' system, based on demand. (ii) is false : while a low batch set-up costs are a prerequisite for successful JIT, the use of JIT will result in smaller batches, more set-ups and hence higher set up costs overall. (iii) is true. JIT needs multifunctional workers, who could be grouped by products rather than tasks.

**19 D**

Product return per minute = (selling price − direct material cost)/time on bottleneck resource = $(45 − 14)/10 = $3.10

**20 D**

|  | J | K | L | M |
|---|---|---|---|---|
|  | $ | $ | $ | $ |
| Selling price | 2,000 | 1,500 | 1,500 | 1,750 |
| Direct materials | 410 | 200 | 300 | 400 |
| Throughput | 1,590 | 1,300 | 1,200 | 1,350 |
| Minutes on Machine X | 120 | 100 | 70 | 110 |
| Throughput per minute | $13.25 | $13.00 | $17.14 | $12.27 |
| Ranking | 2 | 3 | 1 | 4 |

**21 B**

|  | $ |
|---|---|
| Sales revenue: 600 units × $450 | 270,000 |
| Return on investment required: 20% × $300,000 | 60,000 |
| Total cost allowed | 210,000 |
| Target cost per unit: 210,000/600 | 350 |

**22** Processing 70 units of product T will give the larger throughput contribution per day.

|  | Product S | Product T |
|---|---|---|
| Throughput of process X per day | $13.5 \text{ hrs} \times \dfrac{60}{5} = 162.00$ | $13.5 \text{ hrs} \times \dfrac{60}{7.5} = 108.00$ |

(Production time: 15 − 1.5 = 13.5 hrs)

| Throughput of process Y per day | $14 \text{ hrs} \times \dfrac{60}{18} = 46.67$ | $14 \text{ hrs} \times \dfrac{60}{12} = 70.00$ |
|---|---|---|

(Production time : 15 − 1 = 14 hrs)

Process Y limits the production of both products to figures that are less than sales demand.

Throughput contribution per hour of product S: $\dfrac{(\$95.00 - 20.00)}{18} \times 60 = \$250.00$

Throughput contribution per hour of product T: $\dfrac{(\$85.00 - 20.00)}{12} \times 60 = \$325.00$

**23** The average cost per unit is $5,107.20

*Calculation of time per unit:*

| 1 unit takes: | 80 hours |
|---|---|
| 2 units take: 80% × 80 | 64 hours |
| 4 units take: 80% × 64 | 51.2 hours |
| 8 units take: 80% × 51.2 | 40.96 hours |

*Cost per unit:*

|  |  | $ |
|---|---|---|
| Labour cost | 40.96 hours × $7.50 | 307.20 |
| Direct material cost |  | 4,000.00 |
| Fixed costs ($6,400/8) |  | 800.00 |
|  |  | ———— |
|  |  | 5,107.20 |
|  |  | ———— |

**24** 9.98 minutes is the time taken for the 4th unit.

Using the learning curve model $Y = ax^b$

b = log 0.8/log 2 = −0.3219

|  | Cumulative average minutes | Total minutes |
|---|---|---|
| For the 3rd unit | $Y = 22 \times 3^{-0.3219} = 15.45$ | $\times 3 \quad = 46.34$ |
| For the 4th unit | $Y = 22 \times 4^{-0.3219} = 14.08$ | $\times 4 \quad = 56.32$ |

Therefore the time for the 4th unit is 56.32 − 46.34 = 9.98 minutes.

**25** **D**

A product's life cycle costs are very inclusive; none of these would be excluded.

**26  D**

|  | J | H | K |
|---|---|---|---|
|  | $ | $ | $ |
| Gross margin | 2,000,000 | 3,000,000 | 2,500,000 |
| Sales visits at $400 | 62,400 | 68,800 | 83,200 |
| Order processing at $50 | 75,000 | 75,000 | 100,000 |
| Despatch at $150 | 225,000 | 225,000 | 300,000 |
| Billing and collection at $150 | 450,000 | 450,000 | 600,000 |
| Total | 812,400 | 818,800 | 1,083,200 |
| Net profit/(loss) per customer | 1,187,600 | 2,181,200 | 1,416,800 |
| Ranking | 3 | 1 | 2 |

**27  D**

It is worth noting that the labour cost is not needed here: it is a direct cost and will not change, regardless of the method used. We will calculate the overhead cost per unit under both systems and calculate the difference.

AC: since the time per unit is the same for each product, the overheads per unit will also be the same.

$156,000/6,000 units = $26 (we would get the same answer using labour hours)

| ABC: | Number of deliveries for X | 1,000/200 | = 5 |
|---|---|---|---|
|  | Number of deliveries for Y | 2,000/400 | = 5 |
|  | Number of deliveries for Z | 3,000/1,000 | = 3 |
|  | Total |  | = 13 |

Cost per delivery   $156,000/13 = $12,000

Cost per unit of Z: ($12,000 per deliver x 3 deliveries) / (Total units required 3,000 units) = $12

Decrease          $26 – $12 = $14

**28  TPAR = 1.50**

The return per factory hour = ($100 – $40)/3.75 hours = $16

Factory costs per factory hour = ($10 + $30)/3.75 hours = $10.67

Throughput accounting ratio = Return per factory hour/cost per factory hour = $16/$10.67 = 1.50.

**29  C**

Unit, batch, product and facility all relate to levels of activity, while value added and non value added relate to the type of activity.

**30   C**

Statement (i) provides a definition of a cost driver. Cost drivers for long-term variable overhead costs will be the volume of a particular activity to which the cost driver relates, so Statement (ii) is correct. Statement (iii) is also correct. In traditional absorption costing, standard high-volume products receive a higher amount of overhead costs than with ABC. ABC allows for the unusually high costs of support activities for low-volume products (such as relatively higher set-up costs, order processing costs and so on).

**31**   The answer is $7.50

Number of batches per product given by total production units/batch size

Product X    number of batches = 15/2.5 = 6
Product Y    number of batches = 25/5 = 5
Product Z    number of batches = 20/4 = 5

Total number of batches = 16

Machine set up costs attributed to products in same ratio as number of batches

Set up costs for product Y = 5/16 × $600,000 = $187,500

Since there are 25,000 units of Y in total, the machine set-up costs that would be attributed to each unit of Product Y is $187,500 / 25,000 units = $7.50.

**32   A**

| Cost | Classification |
|---|---|
| (i) | Facility-sustaining |
| (ii) | Facility-sustaining |
| (iii) | Product-sustaining |
| (iv) | Product-sustaining |
| (v) | Facility-sustaining |

**33**

| Washing | 1,200 × (60/6) | = | 12,000 units |
|---|---|---|---|
| Filling | 700 × (60/3) | = | 14,000 units |
| Capping | 250 × (60/1.5) | = | 10,000 units |
| Labelling | 450 × (60/2) | = | 13,500 units |
| Packing | 1,300 × (60/6) | = | 13,000 units |

Maximum output is therefore limited by the capping process to 10,000 units.

| | | = | $0.60 − $0.18 | | = | $0.42 |
|---|---|---|---|---|---|---|
| Throughput per unit | | | | | | |
| Time on bottleneck | = | 1.5/60 | | | = | 0.025 of an hour |
| Return per hour | = | $0.42/0.025 | | | = | $16.80 |
| Total factory cost | = | $4,120 + $0.02 × 10,000 | | | = | $4,320 |
| Cost per hour | = | $4,320/250 hours | | | = | $17.28 per hr |
| TA ratio | = | 16.80/17.28 | | | = | 0.97 |

**34**   **The average time is 216 hours.**

| Units | Average time per unit | Total hours |
|---|---|---|
| 1 | 300 | 300 |
| 2 | 270 | 540 |
| 4 | 243 | 972 |

Average hours per unit for units 3 and 4 = (972 – 540) ÷ 2 = 216 hours.

**35**   All are true. Since quality is customer defined, everyone should become customer focused. Standard costing implies that there is a standard that is good enough, TQM is based on continuous improvement. Last, quality control departments are believed to reinforce the idea that quality is someone else's problem; With TQM, quality is incorporated in everyone's targets.

**36**   Purchasing costs will increase due to the extra requirements applied to suppliers. Stockholding costs will reduce due to lower stock levels. Ordering costs will increase due to the greater specification required, and the increased number of small deliveries. Switching from a traditional inventory ordering system to a just-in-time ordering system would result in increased information system costs in the short term at least, because of implementation, training and upgrade costs of the systems.

**37**   **C**

A is not correct: unless there is a quality programme of some type, a company cannot afford  to have low stocks, in case defective items need to be replaced from stock. B is not rue either: whilst TQM can be used by service companies, it is also seen in manufacturing and other productive industries along with JIT. Statement C is closely related to the truth; customer satisfaction as regards quality and delivery times. D is not right because a TQM system is more concerned with ensuring that errors do not occur in the first place. Any checking of items can be undertaken during the production process itself.

**38**   **A**

The resale value is normally referred to as the 'exchange value'.

**39**   **A**

Batch production uses stocks to supply customers whilst other products are being produced. Stocks are avoided in a JIT system. **Jobbing production** makes products to customer order and is ideal for JIT. **Process production** produces continuous output, and as long as the speed of production can be regulated, this can be tailored to customer requirements. **Services** are always produced just in time, as they cannot be stored.

**40**   **B**

(i) should help to prevent failures. (ii) is the cost of a quality failure discovered externally (it has been returned). (iii) represents appraising the current production and (iv) is the cost of a quality failure discovered internally.

**41**    Value analysis is an examination of the factors affecting the cost of a product or service with the objective of achieving the specified purpose most economically at the required level of quality and reliability.

Functional analysis is an analysis of the relationships between product functions, the cost of their provision and their perceived value to the customer.

Therefore, value analysis is a form of cost reduction which is based upon investigating the processes involved in providing a product or service, whereas functional analysis focuses on the value to the customer of each function of the product or service and from this determines whether it is necessary to reduce the cost of providing each function.

**42**    **B**

**43**    The extended value chain includes both internal and external factors whereas the value chain includes only the internal factors. The value chain is the sequence of business factors that add value to the organisation's products and services and comprises the following:

- Research and Development (R&D)

- Design

- Production

- Marketing

- Distribution

- Customer service

The extended value chain adds suppliers to the left hand side and customers to the right hand side and recognises the importance of the relationships that the organisation has with these external parties in the overall process of adding value.

**44**    Just-in-Time, like so many modern management techniques, places great importance on the 'continuous improvement' ethos. Cost containment will often aim to achieve a pre-determined target, but this target may often remain static over a long period of time. With modern techniques, the target is regularly updated and made more stringent.

Continual cost reduction can be seen in many areas of JIT:

- Reduction in stock levels – large amounts of capital is tied up in high stock levels. Reducing stock levels releases this cash, so that it can be better used elsewhere in the business. Ideally, zero stock should be held.

- Reduction in manufacturing times and customer lead times – the demand based manufacturing of JIT, together with cellular manufacturing enables production times to be greatly reduced. This will improve customer satisfaction and hopefully lead to increased business volume.

- Cross-training of staff: new production methods necessitate staff being competent in several tasks. This may lead to fewer staff being required hence costs are reduced.

**45**

| Costs associated with stopping the output of products which fail to conform to the specifications. **Prevention costs** | Costs of materials or products that fail to meet specifications **Internal failure costs** |
|---|---|
| Costs arising when poor quality products are delivered to customers. **External failure costs** | Costs associated with ensuring that production meets standards. **Appraisal costs** |

**46**   TPAR = 1.3

The throughput accounting ratio is defined as throughput/total factory costs. Throughput accounting aims to discourage inventory building, so the ratios do not take account of inventory movements.

Throughput = sales − all material costs = $35 × 800 − $13,000 = $15,000

(Note that we use materials purchased instead of materials used.)

Total factory costs = all other production costs = $6,900 + $4,650 = $11,550

TA ratio = $15,000/$11,550 = 1.30.

**47**   15.16 hours for the 16th unit.

Average time for 15 units = $y = a.x^b$

$= 54 × 15^{-0.3219}$

$= 22.584$ hours

Average time for 16 units = $y = ax^b$

$= 54 × 16^{-0.3219}$

$= 22.12$ hours

| Total time for 15 units | $= 22.584 × 15$ | $= 338.76$ hours |
|---|---|---|
| Total time for 16 units | $= 22.12 × 16$ | $= 353.92$ hours |
| Time for 16th unit | | $= 15.16$ hours |

**48**   **A**

The average time for two units is $\dfrac{100 + 70}{2} = 85$ hours. This is 85% of the time for the first unit.

**49** 6.67 minutes to be used for the quotation.

The time taken for the 200th unit is calculated as follows:

At 200 units: $y = 30 \times 200^{-0.2345} = 8.660$
Total time = $8.660 \times 200 =$  1,732.00 minutes

At 199 units: $y = 30 \times 199^{-0.2345} = 8.670$
Total time = $8.670 \times 199 =$  1,725.33 minutes

So 200th unit is  6.67 minutes

**50** **D**

**51** **B**

# B: CONTROL AND PERFORMANCE MANAGEMENT OF RESPONSIBILITY CENTRES

**52** **B**

(i), (ii) and (iii) only. Apportioned head office costs are not controllable by the manager of an investment centre. Discretionary fixed costs (those which do not have to be incurred in the short term, such as advertising and training) are within the manager's control, since they can be increased or reduced at fairly short notice.

The level of inventory in the division is a part of the capital invested in the division, which is usually controllable by the manager of an investment centre. The manager also has control over the revenue from sales within the organisation (transfer prices).

**53** **B**

Cost centres have the lowest degree of autonomy with managers only able to control costs. Profit centres have a higher degree of autonomy as managers can not only control costs, but can also control sales prices and revenue. Investment centres have the highest degree of autonomy as managers can not only control costs and revenues but can also make investment decisions not open to managers in either of the other two centres.

**54** 56%.

It would appear that the company should cease producing product YY since it generates a loss. However, for decision-making, contribution should always be used instead of profit.

If the entire $9,000 of fixed cost is avoidable then the company should cease producing N since it will forego contribution of $5,000 but save fixed costs of $9,000 so being $4,000 better off overall.

If, say, only $4,000 of the fixed costs are avoidable, ceasing production of YY would result in loss of contribution of $5,000 but save fixed costs of $4,000 so the company would be $1,000 worse off. Here they should continue production of YY. Since contribution from YY is $5,000 at a minimum the avoidable fixed cost would have to be $5,000.

As a percentage this is $5,000/$9,000 × 100% = 56%.

**55** Division H should be closed and all other divisions should be kept open.

If a division is closed the company will forego any contribution it was expected to generate but it will save any fixed cost that is incurred specifically by that division (no division, no specific fixed cost!).

Therefore, we must look at contribution with less specific fixed costs for each division to see what will be foregone if the division is closed.

|  | Division T | Division H | Division E |
|---|---|---|---|
|  | $000 | $000 | $000 |
| Contribution | 150 | 120 | 50 |
| Specific fixed costs | (135) | (180) | (45) |
| (80% × 450 = 360, 360/8 × 3, 4, 1) | 15 | (60) | 5 |

So, if Division T were to be closed the company will forego $15,000.

If Division E were closed the company will forego $5,000.

Therefore, both of these divisions should be kept open.

However, if Division H is closed the company will forego $120,000 of contribution but save specific fixed costs of $180,000 – a net saving of $60,000.

So, Division H should be closed.

**56**

| 100 reams @ resale value of $10 | $1,000 |
|---|---|
| 150 reams @ market price of $26 | $3,900 |
|  | $4,900 |

**57** The maximum amount that the company should be prepared to pay an external supplier is $114,000 ($22.80 per unit) and to cover its own cost, the business must produce 214 units, to the nearest.

This question is testing the 'make or buy' decision. The business should choose to do whichever is the cheaper of the two options.

If component D12 is purchased from an external supplier, the maximum it should be prepared to pay is equal to the cost it would incur in making the component itself.

Making component D12 itself cost the business $21.00 per unit (this being the marginal cost of making each unit). If the component were not manufactured in-house the avoidable fixed costs of $9,000 would not be incurred.

So cost of manufacturing 5,000 units of D12 = $9,000 + $21.00 × 5,000 = $114,000.

This is therefore the maximum amount that the company should be prepared to pay an external supplier.

If the component D12 is bought-in at a cost of $25 per unit, the contribution made by the business from each unit if F45 sold will be:

|  | $ |
|---|---|
| Selling price | 146 |
| Less: | |
| Variable costs (includes the $25 for component D12) | (62) |
| | ‾‾‾‾ |
| Contribution | 84 |
| | ‾‾‾‾ |

The avoidable fixed costs associated with making F45 are $18,000.

(The question asked for the number of units of product F45 that must be sold to cover its own costs without contributing to T plc's non-avoidable fixed costs, that is, to cover the avoidable fixed costs only.)

To cover this cost the business must produce the following number of units of F45:

$18,000/$84 = 214.29 units. So, 214 units to the nearest.

**58    E**

By setting up your own business you will be giving up the *opportunity* to earn $25,000 per annum. The salary is therefore an opportunity cost. By taking on the rent of the business unit you will be increasing your cost base – so the rent is an incremental cost.

A committed cost is a cost which the new business is already obliged to pay (perhaps for contractual reasons). Sunk costs are past costs. Irrelevant costs are those that have no bearing on the decision to be taken.

**59**    If the contract were to go ahead, five new employees will have to be recruited at an incremental cost of 5 × $45,000 = $225,000 per annum.

This cost would only be for six months.

So cost to the contract would be: $225,000 × 0.5 = $112,500

The cost of the project manager is irrelevant since he already works for Rightlight Ltd. His salary is therefore a committed cost – even the 30% of time he will spend on the contract!

The 'Environmental Awareness' training programme would cost:

5 employees × $3,000 × 80% = $12,000

So total relevant cost if Rightlight Ltd were to run the campaign would be:

$112,500 + $12,000 = $124,500

Instead, Rightlight Ltd could subcontract the work at a cost of $135,000.

The cheaper option is to employ and train the five new employees. Hence, relevant cost of labour for the contract is $124,500.

**60** The ratio is at its lowest when debtors are low and creditors high. Thus the debtors ($135,000) must be double the combined overdraft and creditors (i.e. $67,500).

O/d = $67,500 – $22,000 = $45,500.

Or using algebra, 135,000 = 2(22,000 + o/d)

  67,500 = 22,000 + o/d

    o/d = 45,500.

**61** You need to know the relationship between these ratios. Return on investment = net profit margin × asset turnover

Thus Net profit margin = return on investment ÷ asset turnover

= 18%/2 = 9%.

**62** **B**

The manager of a profit centre can exercise control over revenues and controllable costs, but has no influence concerning the capital invested in the centre.

Contribution (i) would be a useful performance measure because a profit centre manager can exercise control over sales revenue and variable costs. Controllable profit (ii) would also be useful as long as any overhead costs charged in deriving the profit figure are controllable by the profit centre manager. Apportioned central costs would not be deducted when calculating controllable profit. Return on investment (iii), residual income (iv) and economic value added (v) would not be useful because they require a measure of the capital invested in the division.

**63** Remember that the current ratio is current assets/current liabilities.

Here the only liabilities seem to be creditors = $144,000

Current assets must be 1.7 × 144,000 = 244,800

Bank must be 244,800 – 14,800 – 19,600 = 210,400.

**64** You need to know the relationship between these ratios.

Return on investment = net profit margin × asset turnover

    = 16% × 0.9

    = 14.4%.

**65** Return on investment = Asset turnover × Net profit margin.

Therefore ROI = 5 × 4% = 20%

ROI also = Operating profit/Capital employed

$$0.2 = \frac{£80,000}{x}$$

x = $400,000

**66**

| | | |
|---|---|---|
| The operating profit margin for the budget period | 16.5 | % |
| The total net asset turnover for the period | 2.05 | times |
| The budgeted current ratio | 2.03 | times |
| The budgeted quick (acid test) ratio | 0.97 | times |

Operating profit margin = 900/5,440 × 100% =     16.5%

| | $000 | $000 |
|---|---|---|
| Non-current assets | | 1,850 |
| Current assets | | |
| Inventory | 825 | |
| Receivables | 710 | |
| Bank | 50 | |
| | | 1,585 |
| | | 3,435 |
| Less current liabilities | | (780) |
| | | 2,655 |

Net asset turnover = 5,440/2,655 = 2.05 times

Current ratio = 1,585/780 = 2.03 times;  Acid test/quick ratio = (1,585 − 825)/780 = 0.97 times

**67**     DB Holdings Ltd – key business metrics

| | 2013 | 2014 |
|---|---|---|
| ROCE (Operating profit/Capital employed) | 6.72 | 10.00 |
| Operating profit margin (Operating profit/Revenue) | 6.67 | 7.24 |
| Current liquidity ratio (Current assets/Current liabilities) | 3.7 | 2.1* |
| Receivables days (Receivable/Sales) | 24 | 62 |
| Inventory days (Inventory/Purchases**) | 46 | 73 |
| Payable days (Payables/Purchases**) | 23 | 53 |
| Cash conversion period | 47 | 82 |

(Inventory days + receivables days – payables days)

*Note that the overdraft in 2014 means that the company liabilities amount to 180 + 780 = 960

**Approximated as Sales – Operating profit

Note that

- In certain cases an approximate figure is used. For example, in calculating inventory days and payables days one needs to know 'purchases' – but since this is unavailable, operating costs are used instead.

  Operating costs = Sales – Operating profit.

  Since most business costs are purchases, the resultant inventory and payables days figures are meaningful and allow a clear inter-period comparison.

- Inventory and payables days positions for 2013 are both based on year-end figures. Ideally we would base these figures on an average of end 2013 and end 2014 balances. However, these figures are not available, and year-end figures are deemed a suitable approximation.

**68**   The ROI of the investment is $128,000/$855,000 = 15\%$.

Thus the manager's performance will appear to decline if he takes on this project (his new return will fall below the existing 17%). He will therefore reject this investment.

However, a return of 15% is beneficial to the company, and so the manager rejects to the detriment of the company.

**69**   The ROI of the investment is $15,000/$135,000 = 11\%$.

Thus the manager's performance will appear to improve if he takes on this project (his new return will rise above the existing 8%). He will therefore accept this investment.

However, a return of 11% is detrimental to the company, and so the manager accepts to the detriment of the company.

**70**   The ROI of the investment is $28,000/$155,000 = 18\%$.

This will reduce the division's ROI and will cause the manager to reject.

The RI is $28,000 – 15\% \times $155,000 = $4,750$.

Since this is positive the manager will accept.

**71**   **A**

It is worth noting that you do not need the figures to work this question out (although you can use them if you want).

(i)   Paying now would reduce creditors and thus increase capital employed, leading to lower rates of return. Note that the "return" of 5% is nowhere near high enough to make this worth considering.

(ii)   Scrapping will reduce the capital employed, leading to higher returns, the income will just accentuate this.

**72**   Each manager will only consider costs that are variable to him, fixed costs will be ignored – they are unavoidable.

Manager A will want to produce as the transfer price ($12) exceeds his variable cost ($10), adding to his contribution.

Manager B will want to produce as the revenue from the sale ($21) exceeds the variable cost and transfer price ($8 + $12), adding to his contribution.

The company will increase its contribution if production occurs, because the final selling price is greater than the total variable costs.

The position is goal congruent since both divisions wish to produce.

**73**   **B**

The internal price is just another name for the TP, so it is not a method of transfer pricing.

**74**   You must set a price high enough for TM to cover its costs, but not so high that RM cannot make a profit.

For TM, an item sold externally has VC of 60% × $24.00 = $14.40

Of this, $1.50 will not be incurred on an internal transfer so it is not relevant here, VC on internal transfer = $14.40 – $1.50 = $12.90

We do not know RM's cost structure, so we leave the price at $12.90; this will ensure that RM is not discouraged from taking an internal transfer when it is profitable to do so.

**75**

(i)    A can sell all of its output into the intermediate market at $180, so the TP needs to exceed this.

B needs to make a contribution so the TP needs to be below $290 – $80 = $210

So, $180 to $210 range.

(ii)   A needs to cover its costs, so TP must exceed $150.

B can buy from the intermediate market at $180, so the TP must be lower than this.

So, $150 to $180 range.

**76**   **D**

Divisional managers will be more aware of changes in the environment in which their own part of the business operates. Thus a decentralised organisation can respond more rapidly to local environmental changes than can a centralised organisation.

A problem with decentralisation tends to be that managers will give priority to the performance of their own centre, even if an improvement in their own performance can cause a worse performance for the organisation overall. Goal congruence can be difficult to achieve in a decentralised organisation and option A is therefore incorrect.

The selection of non-subjective performance measures can be a problem in a decentralised organisation, therefore option B is incorrect.

Communication can be difficult in a decentralised organisation, especially if the various divisions are geographically widespread. Therefore option C is incorrect.

**77**  18.7%

Return on investment = profit before interest and tax (PBIT)/capital employed

PBIT = $320,000 + $200,000 + $100,000 + $70,000 = $690,000

Capital employed = $2.69m + $1.00m = $3.69m

ROI = 690,000/3,690,000 × 100% = 18.7%

**78**  **B**

| | | | | |
|---|---|---|---|---|
| Original profit | = | $2,000,000 × 12% | = | $240,000 |
| New profit | = | $240,000 + $90,000 | = | $330,000 |
| New capital employed | = | $2,000,000 + $500,000 | = | $2,500,000 |
| Residual income | = | $330,000 − (10% × $2,500,000) | = | $80,000 |

**79**  **C**

| | | | | |
|---|---|---|---|---|
| ROI before project | = | 360/1,600 | = | 22.5% |
| ROI after project | = | 385/(1,600 + 130) | = | 22.3% |

Therefore management would reject this project, if ROI is used as an evaluation criterion.

| | | | | |
|---|---|---|---|---|
| Residual value before project | = | 360 − (1,600 × 0.18) | = | $72,000 |
| Residual value after project | = | 385 − (1,730 × 0.18) | = | $73,600 |

Therefore management would accept this project if residual income is used as an evaluation criterion.

**80**  **C**

$$ROI = \frac{\text{Profit before interest and tax}}{\text{Operations management capital employed}}$$

Profit before interest and tax is the reported profit of the division calculated by 'normal' accounting rules, based only on controllable figures.

The operations management capital employed is the capital employed for which the centre manager is responsible and accountable.

Capital employed can be calculated as equity + long-term debt or non-current assets + current assets − current liabilities.

$$ROI = \frac{400}{1,000 + 700} \quad \text{or} \quad \frac{400}{1,500 + 600 - 400} = 23.5\%$$

**81    B**

|                                     | $000 |
|-------------------------------------|------|
| Profit before interest and tax      | 400  |
| Imputed interest                    |      |
| 12% × 1,700                          | 204  |
|                                     | 196  |

The imputed interest is the cost of capital × capital employed.

**82**    Controllable profit would be calculated before a charge is made for allocated central costs, over which the division manager cannot exercise control.

Controllable profit   =    $(35,000 + 25,000) = $60,000

Controllable ROI without the new machine = $60,000/$420,000 = 14.3%

Controllable ROI with the new machine = $(60,000 + 5,500)/(420,000 + 50,000) = 13.9%

| **Residual income calculations** | *Without machine* | *With machine* |
|----------------------------------|-------------------|----------------|
|                                  | $                 | $              |
| Controllable profit              | 60,000            | 65,500         |
| Interest charge                  | 42,000            | 47,000         |
| Residual income                  | 18,000            | 18,500         |

**83    A**

|                                                   | $        |
|---------------------------------------------------|----------|
| Accounting profit                                 | 135,000  |
| Less additional depreciation (41,000 – 22,000)    | (19,000) |
| Add back increase in doubtful debt provision      | 8,000    |
| NOPAT (ignoring tax)                              | 124,000  |
| Replacement cost of net assets                    | 660,000  |
| Add provision for doubtful debts                  | 12,000   |
| Economic value of capital employed               | 672,000  |
| Cost of capital                                   | × 14%    |
| Capital charge                                    | 94,080   |
| NOPAT                                             | 124,000  |
| Capital charge                                    | 94,080   |
| EVA                                               | 29,920   |

**84    D**

|                                          | $ million |
|------------------------------------------|-----------|
| Operating profit                         | 20.2      |
| Add back launch costs                    | 3.0       |
| Less amortisation of launch costs        | (1.0)     |
|                                          | 22.2      |
| Replacement cost of assets               | 84.0      |
| Add increase in capitalised launch costs | 2.0       |
|                                          | 86.0      |
| Cost of capital                          | × 11%     |
| Capital charge                           | 9.46      |

EVA = $(22.2 − 9.46) million = $12.74 million

**85**

(i)    Operating profit margin          (3,629,156/7,055,016) × 100 = 51.44%
       = operating profit/sales × 100%

(ii)   Capital employed =               4,582,000 + 4,619,582 + 442,443 − 949,339
       total assets − current liabilities    − 464,692 = 8,229,994

       Return on capital employed =
       Operating profit/capital employed
       × 100%                           (3,629,156/8,229,994) × 100 = 44.10%

(iii)  Trade receivable days =          (442,443/7,055,016) × 365 days
       trade receivables/turnover × 365   = 22.89 days

(iv)   Current/liquidity ratio          (4,619,582 + 442,443)/
       = current assets/current liabilities   (949,339 + 464,692) = 3.58:1

**86    D**

An investment centre has responsibility for sales, costs and net assets.

**87  B**

|  | Centre 1 |  | Centre 2 |  |
|---|---|---|---|---|
|  | $ |  | $ | $ |
| External sales (300 × $28) | 8,400 | (150 × $40) |  | 6,000 |
| Transfer sales (150 × $(20 + 20%)) | 3,600 |  |  | – |
|  | 12,000 |  |  | 6,000 |
| Transfer costs |  |  | 3,600 |  |
| Own costs (450 × $20) | 9,000 | (150 × $8) | 1,200 |  |
|  |  |  |  | 4,800 |
| Profit | 3,000 |  |  | 1,200 |

**88  C**

Statement (i) is correct. The buying profit centre will incur the same cost when buying from within and outside the business, and so is likely to be indifferent about the source of supply.

Statement (ii) is correct. When there is spare capacity, a transfer price based on incremental cost rather than market price might encourage the buying profit centre to purchase internally in order to utilise spare capacity. A transfer price based on the full market price will not encourage the utilisation of spare capacity to make a marginal additional profit.

**89**  The annual reduction in divisional profit for Division A amounts to $

> **45,000**

The annual reduction in profit for Company X amounts to $

> **32,500**

Division A will lose the contribution from internal transfers to Division B.

| Contribution forgone | = | 2,500 × $(40 – 22) |
|---|---|---|
|  | = | **$45,000** reduction in profit |

|  | $ per unit |
|---|---|
| Cost per unit from external supplier | 35 |
| Variable cost of internal manufacture saved | 22 |
| Incremental cost of external purchase | 13 |

| Reduction in profit of X | = | $13 × 2,500 units |
|---|---|---|
|  | = | **$32,500** |

**90    C**

The optimum transfer price is where:

Transfer price                        =        marginal cost + opportunity cost

The opportunity cost is the contribution forgone from an external sale of alpha = $16

$(6 + 4 + 2) = $4

The optimum transfer price is therefore:

marginal cost $10 + opportunity cost $4 = $14 per unit

**91    A**

Marginal cost will be same as Variable cost, that is $15.

The two-part tariff transfer price per unit is marginal cost $15.

**92    C**

(i)     *Two-part tariff system*:  The price **per unit** credited to the supplying Division S would be the marginal cost of $28. The agreed fixed fee should be ignored when calculating the **unit** price.

(ii)    *Dual price*: The price credited to the supplying Division S would be the market price $40. (The element of profit in this ($12) would be removed so that only $28 (the marginal cost) would be debited to Division T.)

**93    D**

|                                                          | $   |
| -------------------------------------------------------- | --- |
| Market price of product N in Canada                      | 300 |
| Less:  Total cost                                        | 120 |
|                                                          |     |
| Pre-tax profit                                           | 180 |
| Post-tax profit per unit ($1,100,000/11,000 units)       | 100 |
|                                                          |     |
| Tax (balancing figure)                                   | 80  |

Tax as a percentage of pre-tax profit is $80/$180 × 100 = 44%.

**94 D**

| | Per unit £ | Per unit £ |
|---|---|---|
| Market price in UK | | 250.0 |
| Less: Transfer price at variable cost: $\dfrac{\$120 \times 0.75}{1.5}$ | 60.0 | |
| UK marketing and distribution costs | 40.0 | 100.0 |
| | | 150.0 |
| Less: Tax at 25% | | (37.5) |
| | | 112.5 |

11,000 units at £112.50 = £1,237,500 profit after tax.

**95 A**

A higher transfer price will mean that CMW Ltd is charged more for goods transferred, thus decreasing UK profits and increasing the overseas profit.

Increased royalty payments paid by CMW Ltd will decrease UK profits and increase the overseas profit.

**96** (i) Loss is $1,000,000:

Marginal (variable) cost = 70 + 20 + 10 = $100

External selling price = 150 × 1.3333 = $200

| | | $000 |
|---|---|---|
| Sales | | |
| Internal | 60,000 × $100 | 6,000 |
| External | 40,000 × $200 | 8,000 |
| | | 14,000 |
| Variable cost | 100,000 × $100 | 10,000 |
| Contribution | | 4,000 |
| Fixed costs | | |
| Production | 100,000 × $40 | 4,000 |
| Administration | 100,000 × $10 | 1,000 |
| Loss | | (1,000) |

(ii) Profit is $1,400,000.

The total production cost = $140 (not $150 as this includes selling and administration overhead). This means that sales revenue increases by $40 × 60,000 = $2,400,000 and costs stay the same. Profit is now (1,000,000) + 2,400,000 = $1,400,000.

**97** The level of sales that would maximise the profit from this service for the Legal Division is 2,000 hours and its contribution would be $30,000.

The level of sales that would maximise the profit from L&S for the KL Company as a whole is 3,000 hours and the contribution would be $75,000.

We are trying to maximise the profit from the service from the Legal Division's point of view. As far as the Legal Division is concerned its variable costs are $65 ($25 + $40).

| Hours sold | Price per hour | Variable cost per hour | Contribution per hour | Total contribution |
|---|---|---|---|---|
| 0 | 100 | 65 | 35 | 0 |
| 1,000 | 90 | 65 | 25 | 25,000 |
| 2,000 | 80 | 65 | 15 | 30,000 |
| 3,000 | 70 | 65 | 5 | 15,000 |
| 4,000 | 60 | 65 | (5) | (20,000) |
| 5,000 | 50 | 65 | (15) | (75,000) |

The level of sales that would maximise the contribution for the Legal Division is 2,000 hours and its contribution would be $30,000.

We are trying to maximise the profit from the service from the group point of view. As far as the group is concerned the variable cost of the service is $45 ($20 + $25).

| Hours sold | Price per hour | Variable cost per hour | Contribution per hour | Total contribution |
|---|---|---|---|---|
| 0 | 100 | 45 | 55 | 0 |
| 1,000 | 90 | 45 | 45 | 45,000 |
| 2,000 | 80 | 45 | 35 | 70,000 |
| 3,000 | 70 | 45 | 25 | 75,000 |
| 4,000 | 60 | 45 | 15 | 60,000 |
| 5,000 | 50 | 45 | 5 | 25,000 |

The level of sales that would maximise the contribution for the whole company is 3,000 hours and the contribution would be $75,000.

This answer assumes that the Secretarial Division has spare capacity.

**98** **A**

ROI = Net income/Net assets = 300,000/6,750,000 × 100% = 4.44%

**99** **D**

$300,000 − 13% × $6,750,000 = ($577,000)

**100  A**

EVA = NOPAT − Economic value of assets × Cost of capital

| NOPAT | $m |
|---|---|
| Operating profit | 89.2 |
| Add back development costs | +9.6 |
| Less amortisation of development costs | −3.2 |
| Add back accounting depreciation | +24 |
| Less economic depreciation | −33.6 |
| | 86 |

| Economic value of assets | $m |
|---|---|
| Replacement cost of assets | 168 |
| Less economic depreciation | −33.6 |
| Add net increase in development costs | +6.4 |
| Add working capital | +27.2 |
| | 168 |

EVA = 86 − 13% × 168 = $64.16m

**101**  The post-tax profit for X is $483,000 and the post-tax profit for Y is $669,200.

The variable cost of the component = $600 × 0.6 = $360

Transfer price = $360 × 1.7 = $612

| $000 | X | Y |
|---|---|---|
| Sales: External (W1) | 8,000 | 14,400 |
| Internal (W2) | 7,344 | |
| | 15,344 | 14,400 |
| Variable cost (W3) | (7,920) | (12,144) |
| Fixed production cost (W4) | (5,280) | |
| Fixed non-production cost | (1,500) | (1,300) |
| Profit before tax | 644 | 956 |
| Tax | (161) | (286.8) |
| Profit after tax | 483 | 669.2 |

**Workings**

(W1)  $800 × 10,000 = $8,000,000

$1,200 × 12,000 = $14,400,000

(W2)  12,000 × $612 = $7,344,000

(W3)  $360 × 22,000 = $7,920,000

Variable cost for product W = $400 + $612 = $1,012 per unit

$1,012 × 12,000 = $12,144,000

(W4)  $240 × 22,000 = $5,280,000

**102**  The two correct statements are Option 2 'It is commonly used and understood' and option 6 'It can be used to compare projects of different sizes'.

Option 1 is not correct – it is a percentage not an absolute value. Option 3 is not correct – profits are subjective not objective, depending on the accounting policies used. Option 4 is not correct – it is not linked to the overall company cost of capital, so can give non goal congruent decisions and option 5 is not correct– it uses profits, which can be manipulated to change the ROI.

**103**  The answer is 10.25%. We need to add back the non-controllable head office depreciation and the non-controllable financing costs but not the controllable depreciation on X's assets to get the profit figure.

**104**  Only statement iv is correct. i projects with a positive NPV should always be accepted (ignoring risk); ii profit centres will not be in control of their investment of capital so shouldn't be evaluated on its use; iii Tax is not controllable so shouldn't be included in the calculation of ROI.

**105  D**

Project ROI: Average annual profits = revenue – variable costs – depreciation

Revenue = $20,000*12 = $240,000

Variable costs = $5,000*12 = $60,000

Depreciation = ($600,000 – $100,000)/5 = $100,000

Annual profit = $240,000 – $60,000 – $100,000 = $80,000

Initial investment less 1 year's depreciation = $600,000 – $100,000 = $500,000

ROI = $80,000/$500,000*100 = 16%

Dilutes the existing ROI so would not be accepted.

ROI is not related to cost of capital for evaluation. Plus the cost of capital isn't given, so we couldn't evaluate on that basis.

Evaluating the ROI without the depreciation figure (i.e. using cash flows instead of profits) would give an answer of 36% (or 30% if depreciation isn't deducted from capital to get NBV) which is incorrect as we need to use profits, not cash flows.

**106** 22%

Profits = annual cash flows – depreciation

Here, depreciation = ($50,000 – $5,000)/5 years = $9,000 per annum.

Annual profits = $20,000 – $9,000 = $11,000

ROI = Annual profits / Capital employed

ROI = ($11,000 / $50,000) × 100%

ROI = 22%

**Tutorial note**

*Note that we assume that the 'Capital Employed' at the start of the year (i.e. before depreciation is deducted) is the one that was used to generate the profits at the end of the year. Therefore, the opening capital employed is generally used in OT calculations, unless the question directs you otherwise.*

**107** Options 1 and 4 are correct. Profits are subjective rather than objective (as they depend on the accounting policies used) and can be manipulated. As an absolute measure, Residual Income can't be used to compare different sized investments.

**108** **B**

Current profit can be calculated as 0.2 × $1.2 m = $240,000

Current profit + Project A (highest ROI > 20%):

ROI = (240 + 100)/(1,200 + 300) = 22.66%

Current profit + Projects A and B (ROI > 22.66%):

ROI = (240 + 100 + 210)/(1,200 + 300 + 700) = 25%

Current profit + Projects A, B and C (ROI > 25%):

ROI = (240 + 100 + 210 + 130)/(1,200 + 300 + 700 + 500) = 25.2%, so we shouldn't add N as ROI < 25.2%

**109** **B**

Net monthly cash = $7,500 – $4,900 = $2,600

Net annual cash flow = $2,600 × 12 months = $31,200

Annual depreciation = ($100,000 – $10,000)/5 years = $18,000

Annual profit = $31,200 – $18,000 = $13,200

Notional interest charge = $100,000 × 12% = $12,000

Residual income = $13,200 – $12,000 = $1,200

RI is positive so accept.

Bonus is based on RI so irrelevant whether project makes profit or not. ROI is irrelevant.

**110** Statements (i) and (iv) apply.

Statements (ii) and (iii) do not apply: ROI does not relate profitability to the cost of capital, and RI is an absolute measure so is distorted by divisional size.

**111** The answer is $250,000.

Controllable profits amount to $650,000. Admin recharge and depreciation are not controllable, so we must exclude them. Controllable capital employed $2,000,000; the allocated floor in head office is not a controllable asset, so is excluded.

Controllable RI = $650,000 – ($2,000,000*0.2) = $250,000.

**112** **C**

Project A

incremental contribution $20,000

incremental depreciation $12,500

incremental profit $7,500

project RI = $7,500 – $50,000*13% = $1,000. RI is positive so accept.

Project B

incremental contribution $200,000

incremental depreciation $30,000

incremental profit $170,000

project RI = $170,000 – $1,500,000*13% = $–25,000. RI is negative so reject.

**113** **B**

**114** The balanced scorecard approach is a way of providing information to management which involves the inclusion of non-financial information alongside financial information.

It emphasises the need to provide the user with a set of information which addresses all relevant areas of performance in an objective and unbiased fashion.

Although the specific measures used may vary, a scorecard would normally include the following measures

- profitability – the financial perspective

- customer satisfaction – the customer perspective

- innovation – the innovation and learning perspective

- internal efficiency – the internal business perspective.

By providing all this information in a single report, management is able to assess the impact of particular actions on all perspectives of the company's activities. Under each perspective, a company should state its aims and specify measures of performance.

For example:

|   | | *Aims* | *Measure* |
|---|---|---|---|
| 1 | Financial perspective | Survival | Current ratio |
| 2 | Customer perspective | Satisfaction | Returning customers |
| 3 | Internal business perspective | Efficiency | Throughput rates |
| 4 | Innovation and learning perspective | New products | Income from new products |

**115  C**

**116**  Statement (ii) only is true: the RI will increase, because the additional imputed interest charge will be lower than the additional profit generated.

Statement (i) is false, as the ROI and Residual Income might be used as one of the measures within the financial perspective. Statement (iii) is also false, as the internal business perspective monitors what the business must be good at in order to succeed, for example, the average setup time or the speed with which interdepartmental queries are handled. Statement (iv) is false as a disadvantage of residual income is that it does not facilitate comparisons between investment centres. The same absolute value of RI might be earned by two investment centres but it is much easier for a larger investment centre to generate a given level of RI than it is for a smaller investment centre.

**117**  Beyond Budgeting (BB) is the name given to a body of practices intended to replace budgeting as a management model. The core concept is the need to move from a business model based on centralised organisational hierarchies to one based on devolved networks.

BB is a 'responsibility model' whereby managers are given goals which are based on benchmarks linked variously to world class performance, peers, competitors and/or earlier periods. This requires an adaptive approach whereby authority is devolved to managers.

**118  C**

For every unit of Product B not sold internally, Division A would sell an equally profitable Product A externally, so there would be no change in the profits of Division A. The company as a whole would gain ($176 − $140) = $36 per unit on every unit of product A and pay ($152 − $140) = $12 per unit more on every unit of Product B, so gains overall.

**119  B**

To get a constant ROI, both profits and capital should be constant. Reducing balance depreciation would increase profits over the life. Net book value would decrease the capital figure.

**120**  All statements apply.

## C: LONG-TERM DECISION MAKING

### 121 C

| | $ | Tax saved at 25% | Yr 1 | Yr 2 | Yr 3 |
|---|---|---|---|---|---|
| Cost of asset | 80,000 | | | | |
| Year 1 writing down allowance (20%) | 16,000 | 4,000 | 2,000 | 2,000 | |
| Balance | 64,000 | | | | |
| Year 2 writing down allowance (20%) | 12,800 | 3,200 | | 1,600 | 1,600 |
| | | | | ——— | |
| | | | | 3,600 | |

Cash flows in the second year

| | $ |
|---|---|
| Tax relief on asset | 3,600 |
| Cash inflow | 25,000 |
| Tax due – year 1 cash flow $25,000 × 25% × 0.5 | (3,125) |
| Tax due – year 2 cash flow $25,000 × 25% × 0.5 | (3,125) |
| | ——— |
| | 22,350 |
| Discount factor, year 2 at 5% | 0.907 |
| Present value of cash flows in Year 2 | $20,271 |

### 122 A

Annual cost of capital: 10%

Inflation rate: 4%

Real rate: $(1.10/1.04) - 1 = 0.0577$

| | | |
|---|---|---|
| Year 1 discount rate: | $1/1.0577$ | 0.945 |
| Year 2 discount rate: | $1/(1.0577^2)$ | 0.894 |
| Year 3 discount rate: | $1/(1.0577^3)$ | 0.845 |
| Year 4 discount rate: | $1/(1.0577^4)$ | 0.799 |
| | | ——— |
| | | 3.483 |
| | | ——— |

Annual inflow years 1–4: 6,000 × $12 = $72,000

|  |  |  | Discount rate | $ |
|---|---|---|---|---|
| Year 0 | Investment | $250,000 | 0 | 250,000 |
| Year 1–4 | Inflow | $72,000 | 3.483 | 250,776 |
|  |  |  |  | ———— |
|  | NPV |  |  | $776 i.e. $800 |

Alternatively, you can reach the same solution (with some differences possibly for rounding error) by inflating all the cash flows at 4% to their 'out-turn' amount, and discounting these inflated cash flows at the money cost of capital, 10%. The cash flows would be ($72,000 × 1.04) $74,880 in year 1, $77,875 in year 2, $80,990 in year 3 and $84,230 in year 4.

## 123  B

| Year | Cash inflow/(outflow) | Discount factor @ 8% | Present value $ |
|---|---|---|---|
| 0 | (60,000) | 1.000 | (60,000) |
| 1 | 23,350 | 0.926 | 21,622 |
| 2 | 29,100 | 0.857 | 24,939 |
| 3 | 27,800 | 0.794 | 22,073 |
|  |  |  | ———— |
| Net present value |  |  | 8,634 |

**Workings**

**Cash flows**

| Flow $ | Probability | $ |
|---|---|---|
| Year 1 |  |  |
| 35,000 | 0.25 | 8,750 |
| 20,000 | 0.55 | 11,000 |
| 18,000 | 0.20 | 3,600 |
|  |  | ———— |
| Expected value |  | 23,350 |
|  |  |  |
| Year 2 |  |  |
| 40,000 | 0.25 | 10,000 |
| 26,000 | 0.55 | 14,300 |
| 24,000 | 0.20 | 4,800 |
|  |  | ———— |
| Expected value |  | 29,100 |
|  |  |  |
| Year 3 |  |  |
| 32,000 | 0.25 | 8,000 |
| 28,000 | 0.55 | 15,400 |
| 22,000 | 0.20 | 4,400 |
|  |  | ———— |
| Expected value |  | 27,800 |

**124  A**

Annual cost of capital: 8%

Inflation rate: 3%

Real rate: $(1.08/1.03) - 1 = 0.0485$

| | | |
|---|---|---|
| Year 1 discount rate: | $1/1.0485$ | 0.954 |
| Year 2 discount rate: | $1/(1.0485^2)$ | 0.910 |
| Year 3 discount rate: | $1/(1.0485^3)$ | 0.868 |
| | | 2.732 |

Annual inflow years 1–3: $4,000 \times \$5 = \$20,000$

| | | | Discount rate | $ |
|---|---|---|---|---|
| Year 0 | Investment | $50,000 | 0 | 50,000 |
| Year 1–3 | Inflow | $20,000 | 2.732 | 54,640 |
| | NPV | | | 4,640 i.e. $4,500 |

Alternatively, you can reach the same solution (with some differences possibly for rounding error) by inflating all the cash flows at 3% to their 'out-turn' amount, and discounting these inflated cash flows at the money cost of capital, 8%. The cash flows would be (20,000 × 1.03) $20,600 in year 1, $21,218 in year 2 and $21,855 in year 3.

**125  $60,000**

| Year | Cash ($000) | 17% discount factor | Present value ($000) |
|---|---|---|---|
| 0 | (400) | 1.000 | (400) |
| 1 | 210 | 0.855 | 179.55 |
| 2 | 240 | 0.731 | 175.44 |
| 3 | 320 | 0.624 | 199.68 |
| | | | 154.67 |

Maximum PV of advertising expenditure = $154,670.

Annualise by dividing by annuity factor for years 0 to 2 = 1 + 0.855 + 0.731 = 2.586.

Therefore, maximum cash = $154,670 ÷ 2.586 = $59,811, or $60,000 (rounded to the nearest $000).

**126  $8,503**

NPV = $0

Let $x be annual rent. The annuity factor for year 5 at 17% is 3.199.

∴ $x × 3.199 = 27,200

∴ $x = 8,503

**127** 8.9%

Contribution per annum = $320,000 + $160,000

= $480,000

Contribution per unit = $180 − $60

= $120 per unit

$\therefore$ Level of activity = $\dfrac{\$480,000}{\$120}$ = 4,000 units

NPV can fall by $244,170.

Converted to annual cash equivalent:

= $\dfrac{\$244,170}{3.791}$ = $64,408 per annum

$\therefore$ Unit selling price can fall by up to:

$\dfrac{\$64,408}{4,000 \text{ units}}$ = $16.10 per unit

As a percentage: $\dfrac{\$16.10}{\$180} \times 100$ = 8.9%

**128**

The company's real cost of capital is

| 2.88 | % |

The net present value of the project, when discounting money cash flow at the money rate:

$ | 15,473 |

The net present value of the project, when discounting real cash flow at the real rate:

$ | 15,387 |

**Workings:**

(1 + real rate) = $\dfrac{(1+\text{money rate})}{(1+\text{inflation rate})}$

= $\dfrac{1.07}{1.04}$

= 1.0288

$\therefore$ Real rate = 2.88% per annum.

Discounting money cash flow at the money rate:

| Money cash flow | | Discount factor at 7% | Present value |
|---|---|---|---|
| Yr 0 | (500,000) | 1 | (500,000) |
| Yr 1 | 130,000 × 1.04 = 135,200 | 0.935 | 126,412 |
| Yr 2 | 130,000 × 1.04² = 140,608 | 0.873 | 122,751 |
| Yr 3 | 130,000 × 1.04³ = 146,232 | 0.816 | 119,325 |
| Yr 4 | 130,000 × 1.04⁴ = 152,082 | 0.763 | 116,039 |
| | Net present value | | (15,473) |

Alternatively, discounting real cash flow at the real rate

| | | Discount factor at 7% | Present value |
|---|---|---|---|
| Yr 0 | (500,000) | 1 | (500,000) |
| Yr 1–4 | 130,000 | 3.7278 (W1) | 484,612 |
| | Net present value | | (15,387) |

Annuity factor for a discount rate of 2.88% for four years is calculated using the formula $(1 - (1+0.0288)^4)/0.0288$

## 129 A

This question requires the relationship between money rates and real rates:

$1 + r = 1 + i/1 + h$ where: r = real rate, i = money rate, h = inflation rate.

Rearranged, this gives    $1 + h = 1 + i/1 + r$

$1 + h = 1 + 0.12/1 + 0.06$ so h = 5.66%

## 130 The answer is $17,622.

Capital allowance in Year 2:

| Year | Written down value | Capital allowance | Tax Saving | Cash timing |
|---|---|---|---|---|
| 1 | $75,000 | $25,000 | $7,500 | $3,750 |
| 2 | $56,250 | $18,750 | $5,625 | $3,750 + $2,812.50 |
| | | | | $2,812.50 |

| Year | Capital allowance benefit | Annual cash inflow | Corporation tax | Net cash | Discount factor | Present value |
|---|---|---|---|---|---|---|
| 2 | $6,562.50 | $20,000 | $(6,000) | $20,562.50 | 0.857 | $17,622 |

## 131 C

Profitability index = NPV per $ invested = $140,500/$500,000 = 0.28

**132** $13,112

$$1.11/1.X6 \quad = \quad 1.0472$$

Real rate $\quad = \quad 4.72\%$

$$\frac{1-(1+r)^{-n}}{r}$$

Annuity factor $\quad = \quad \dfrac{1-(1.0472)^{-10}}{0.0472}$

$\quad = \quad 7.8278$

NPV = 40,000 × 7.8278 − 300,000 $\quad = \quad$ $13,112

**133** The internal rate of return of the project is 10% + $\dfrac{\$12,304}{(\$12,304+\$3,216)} \times (15-10)\%$ = 14%

**134** The IRR is approximately 26%

NPV at 10% = $87,980

Discounting the cash flows using a higher discount rate, say 20% gives:

| Year | Cash flow $ | DF | PV $ |
|---|---|---|---|
| 0 | (200,000) | 1.000 | (200,000) |
| 1 | 80,000 | 0.833 | 66,640 |
| 2 | 90,000 | 0.694 | 62,460 |
| 3 | 100,000 | 0.579 | 57,900 |
| 4 | 60,000 | 0.482 | 28,920 |
| 5 | 40,000 | 0.402 | 16,080 |
| | | | **32,000** |

Using the formula:

$$IRR \approx A + (B-A)\frac{N_A}{N_A - N_B}$$

Where $\quad$ A $\quad = \quad$ lower discount rate $\quad$ (10%)

$\quad$ B $\quad = \quad$ higher discount rate $\quad$ (20%)

$\quad$ $N_A$ $\quad = \quad$ NPV at rate A $\quad$ (87,980)

$\quad$ $N_B$ $\quad = \quad$ NPV at rate B $\quad$ (32,000)

IRR (%) = 20 + (10 × 87,980/55,980) = 26%

**135 B**

Profits in Year 1 = $2,000 – depreciation ($60,000/10) = $8,000

Profits in Year 2 = $13,000 – depreciation $6,000 = $7,000

Profits in Year 3 = $23,000 – depreciation $6,000 = $14,000

Profits in Years 4 to 6 = $25,000 – depreciation $6,000 = $19,000

Profits in Years 7 to 10 = $30,000 – depreciation $6,000 = $24,000

Average profits = (–$8,000 + $7,000 + $14,000 + ($19,000 × 3) + (24,000 × 4))/10

Average profits = $16,600

The investment in Year 1 is $60,000 and the investment in Year 10 is nil. The average investment is therefore $60,000/2 = $30,000. The ARR is therefore $16,600/$30,000 = 55%

**136 D**

Statement 1 is false; ARR places equal value on all cash flows throughout a project's life. NPV places less value on later cash flows. Statement 2 is true: the IRR is the rate that equates the present value of inflows with the present value of the initial outflows. If the IRR is greater than the cost of capital, later cash flows would have been discounted too much.

**137**   Payback period for Project A: 3 years 4 months

Discounted payback for Project B: 4.47 years

IRR = 15%

**Workings:**

| Year | $000 | $000 |
|------|------|------|
| 0 | (400) | (400) |
| 1 | 100 | (300) |
| 2 | 120 | (180) |
| 3 | 140 | (40) |
| 4 | 120 | 80 |

Payback period = 3 years + 40/120ths of year 4 = **3.33 years or 3 years 4 months**

Discounted cash flows are:

| Year | $000 | Present value $000 | Cumulative present value $000 |
|------|------|-----|------|
| 0 | (450 × 1) | (450) | (450) |
| 1 | 130 × 0.909 | 118.17 | (331.83) |
| 2 | 130 × 0.826 | 107.38 | (224.45) |
| 3 | 130 × 0.751 | 97.63 | (126.82) |
| 4 | 130 × 0.683 | 88.79 | (38.03) |
| 5 | 130 × 0.621 | 80.73 | 42.70 |

Discounted payback occurs in year 5 and can be estimated as:

4 years plus 38.03/80.73 of year five = 4.47 years

NPV at 10% is given as $48,000 in the question. Since the NPV is positive the IRR must be higher. If we try discounting at 20%:

| Year | Cash flow $000 | Discount factor | Present value $000 |
|---|---|---|---|
| 0 | (350) | 1.000 | (350) |
| 1 | 50 | 0.833 | 42 |
| 2 | 110 | 0.694 | 76 |
| 3 | 130 | 0.579 | 75 |
| 4 | 150 | 0.482 | 72 |
| 5 | 100 | 0.402 | 40 |
| NPV | | | (45) |

IRR = 10% + [48/(48 + 45) × (20 − 10)%] = **15% (approx)**

## 138   C

| Investment | J $000 | K $000 | L $000 | M $000 | N $000 |
|---|---|---|---|---|---|
| Initial investment | 400 | 350 | 450 | 500 | 600 |
| Net present value (NPV) | 125 | 105 | 140 | 160 | 190 |
| Profitability index (NPV per $ invested) | 0.3125 | 0.30 | 0.3111 | 0.32 | 0.3166 |
| Ranking | 3 | 4 | | 1 | 2 |

J would be chosen before L and, as they are mutually exclusive, L can be disregarded.

The optimum investment plan is $500,000 in M and the remaining $500,000 in N.

## 139

| Project | EV $000 | Workings |
|---|---|---|
| L | 500 | (500 × 0.2) + (470 × 0.5) + (550 × 0.3) |
| M | 526 | (400 × 0.2) + (550 × 0.5) + (570 × 0.3) |
| N | 432.5 | (450 × 0.2) + (400 × 0.5) + (475 × 0.3) |
| O | 398 | |
| P | 497.5 | |

Project M will maximise expected cash.

## 140   1.5 years payback period.

Depreciation is not a cash flow so needs to be added back to profit to calculate cash flows.

Depreciation on straight line basis    = ($400,000 − $50,000)/5 = $70,000 per year

| Year | Profit ($) | Cash flow ($) | Cumulative cash flow ($) |
|---|---|---|---|
| 0 | | (400,000) | (400,000) |
| 1 | 175,000 | 245,000 | (155,000) |
| 2 | 225,000 | 295,000 | 140,000 |

Payback period = 1 + 145/295 years = 1.5 years to nearest 0.1 years

**141** The present value of a $1 perpetuity is 1/r; The present value of the rental income is $80,000/0.08 = $1,000,000. Therefore, the NPV of the investment is $1,000,000 − $850,000 = $150,000.

**142 A**

The projects selected should be the combination of projects with the greatest total NPV, subject to the constraint that the total initial outlay must not exceed $570,000. The other constraint is that projects A and E are mutually exclusive.

| Project combination | Total expected NPV | Total outlay |
|---|---|---|
| D, E and F | $18,777 | $510,000 |
| A, B and F | $ 13,225 | $576,000 |
| A, D and F | $ 19,637 | $576,000 |
| A, D and E (*) | $ 20,134 | $606,000 |

(*) This should have been rejected outright, as projects A and E are mutually exclusive.

**143**

| One year replacement cycle | | |
|---|---|---|
| | 0 | 1 |
| Buy asset | $(20,000) | |
| | | |
| Running costs | | $(5,000) |
| Trade-in | | $16,000 |
| Net cash flow | $(20,000) | $11,000 |
| DF @ 10% | 1 | 0.909 |
| PV | $(20,000) | $9,999 |
| NPV | (10,001) | |

The Equivalent Annual Cost can be calculated as $10,001/1 year AF = $10,001/0.909 = $11,002. We may compare this EAC with that of a 2-year replacement cycle below:

| Two year replacement cycle | | | |
|---|---|---|---|
| | 0 | 1 | 2 |
| Buy asset | $(20,000) | | |
| | | | |
| Running costs | | $(5,000) | $(5,500) |
| Trade-in | | | $13,000 |
| Net cash flow | $(20,000) | $(5,000) | $7,500 |
| DF @ 10% | 1 | 0.909 | 0.826 |
| PV | $(20,000) | $(4,545) | 6,195 |
| NPV | (18,350) | | |

The Equivalent Annual Cost can be calculated as $18,350/2 year AF = $18,350/1.736 = $10,570.

This EAC is lower than the 1-year replacement cycle EAC. Therefore, the machine should be replaced after 2 years.

**144** The optimal replacement period is every two years.

| One year replacement cycle | | |
|---|---|---|
| | 0 | 1 |
| Buy asset | $(12,000) | |
| | | |
| Maintenance costs | | $0 |
| Trade-in | | $9,000 |
| Net cash flow | $(12,000) | $9,000 |
| DF @ 15% | 1 | 0.870 |
| PV | $(12,000) | $7,830 |
| NPV | $ (4,170) | |

The Equivalent Annual Cost can be calculated as $4,170/1 year AF = $10,001/0.870 = $4,793. We may compare this EAC with that of a 2-year replacement cycle below:

| Two year replacement cycle | | | |
|---|---|---|---|
| | 0 | 1 | 2 |
| Buy asset | $(12,000) | | |
| | | | |
| Maintenance costs | | $(1,500) | |
| Trade-in | | | $7,500 |
| Net cash flow | $(12,000) | $(1,500) | $7,500 |
| DF @ 15% | 1 | 0.870 | 0.756 |
| PV | $(12,000) | $(1,305) | 5,670 |
| NPV | (7,635) | | |

The Equivalent Annual Cost can be calculated as $7,635/2 year AF = $18,350/1.626 = $4,696. We may compare this EAC with that of a 3-year replacement cycle below:

| Two year replacement cycle | | | | |
|---|---|---|---|---|
| | 0 | 1 | 2 | 3 |
| Buy asset | $(12,000) | | | |
| | | | | |
| Maintenance costs | | $(1,500) | $(2,700) | |
| Trade-in | | | | $7,000 |
| Net cash flow | $(12,000) | $(1,500) | $(2,700) | $7,000 |
| DF @ 15% | 1 | 0.870 | 0.756 | 0.658 |
| PV | $(12,000) | $(1,305) | $(2,041) | $4,606 |
| NPV | $(10,740) | | | |

The Equivalent Annual Cost can be calculated as $10,740/3 year AF = $10,740/2.283 = $4,704.

**145 D**

Equivalent annual cost = (Present value of all costs)/Annuity factor for year 8.

The annuity factor for year 8 (denominator) can be read from the present value and cumulative present value tables, in the 20% column: 3.837 cash flows can be listed as follows:

Initial cost of the machine $150,000, PV $150,000.

Machine resale value $30,000 after 8 years, PV = $30,000 × DF 8@20% so PV = $30,000 × 0.233 = $6,990

Annual running costs $6,000 for the first three years of use : their PV can be calculated as $6,000 × CDF 3 years @ 20% so PV = $6,000 × 2.106 = $12,636

Annual running costs $8,000 for each of the next five years.: their PV can be calculated as $8,000 x(CDF 8 years @ 20% − CDF 3 years @ 20%) so PV = $8,000 x(3.837 − 2.106) = $13,848

Therefore, Equivalent annual cost = −$150,000 + $6,990 − $12,636 − $13,848/AF 3.837

EAC = $44,173, or $44,200 to the nearest $100.

**146 A**

Depreciation must be added back to the annual profit figures to derive the annual cash flows. Annual depreciation = $(110,400 − 9,600)/4 years = $25,200

Adding $25,200 to each year's profit figure produces the following cash flows:

|  | Cash flow $ | Cumulative cash flows $ |
|---|---|---|
| Initial investment | (110,400) | (110,400) |
| Year 1 | 64,800 | (45,600) |
| Year 2 | 44,800 | (800) |
| Year 3 | 47,600 | 43,800 |

Payback period = 2 years + (800/47,600) = 2.01 years

---

**Tutorial note**

*If you selected a payback period of 3.89 years you based your calculations on the accounting profits after the deduction of depreciation. The calculation of the payback period should be based on cash flows.*

---

Accounting rate of return (ARR)

Average profit = $(39,600 + 19,600 + 22,400 + 32,400)/4 = $28,500

Average investment = $(110,400 + 9,600)/2 = $60,000

ARR = $(28,500/60,000) × 100% = 47.5%

---

**Tutorial note**

*If you selected an ARR of 25.8% you calculated the ARR using the opening investment rather than the average investment.*

---

**147  D**

**Net Present Value**

| Year | Cash flow $ | Discount factor 15% | Present value $ |
|---|---|---|---|
| 0 | (12,000) | 1.000 | (12,000) |
| 1 | (4,800) | 0.870 | (4,176) |
| 2 | 16,800 | 0.756 | 12,701 |
| 3 | 14,400 | 0.658 | 9,475 |
| Net Present Value (NPV) | | | 6,000 |

**Tutorial note**

*If you selected an NPV of $4,440 you treated the $12,000 cash flow as occurring in year 1 and discounted it. Cash flows occurring 'now' should not be discounted.*

| Year | Present value (PV) $ | Cumulative PV $ |
|---|---|---|
| 0 | (12,000) | (12,000) |
| 1 | (4,176) | (16,176) |
| 2 | 12,701 | (3,475) |
| 3 | 9,475 | 6,000 |

DPP = 2 years + ((3,475/9,475) × 1 year)
= 2.36 years

**Tutorial note**

*If you selected 2.0 years you calculated the non-discounted payback period.*

**148  C**

IRR is based on discounted cash flow principles. It therefore considers all of the cash flows in a project (A), does not include notional accounting costs such as depreciation (B) and it considers the time value of money (D).  It is not an absolute measure of return, however, as IRR is expressed as a percentage. Two projects can have the same IRR, but very different cash flows.

**149**  The first statement is not true and describes the IRR, not the MIRR; The MIRR measures the economic yield of an investment under the assumption that any cash surpluses are reinvested at the firm's current cost of capital.

**150  D**

|  | $T_0$ | $T_1$ | $T_2$ | $T_3$ | $T_4$ |
|---|---|---|---|---|---|
|  | ($22,500) | $7,500 | $7,500 | $7,400 | $7,300 |
| DF @ 7% | 1 | 0.935 | 0.873 | 0.816 | 0.763 |
| PV of cash flows | ($22,500) | $7,009 | $6,551 | $6,041 | $5,569 |

Present Value of cash flows from Year 1 to Year 4, or 'PVR' = $25,169.88

Present Value of the 'Investment Phase' of the project, or 'PVI' = $22,500

MIRR = $[PVR/PVI]^{1/n} \times (1+re) -1$, where re = the firm's cost of capital.

Here, MIRR = $[\$25,169.88/\$22,500]^{1/4} \times (1+7\%) -1$

MIRR = 10.04%

**151  A**

|  | $T_0$ | $T_1$ | $T_2$ | $T_3$ | $T_4$ |
|---|---|---|---|---|---|
|  | ($67,000) | $20,000 | $19,500 | $19,000 | $19,000 |
| DF @ 9% | 1 | 0.917 | 0.842 | 0.772 | 0.708 |
| PV of cash flows | ($67,000) | $18,349 | $16,413 | $14,671 | $13,460 |

Present Value of cash flows from Year 1 to Year 4, or 'PVR' = $62,892.95

Present Value of the 'Investment Phase' of the project, or 'PVI' = $67,000

MIRR = $[PVR/PVI]^{1/n} \times (1+re) -1$, where re = the firm's cost of capital.

Here, MIRR = $[\$62,892.95/\$67,000]^{1/4} \times (1+9\%) -1$

MIRR = 7.29%

**152  A**

|  | $T_0$ | $T_1$ | $T_2$ | $T_3$ | $T_4$ |
|---|---|---|---|---|---|
|  | ($120,000) | $45,000 | $35,000 | $35,000 | $30,000 |
| DF @ 6% | 1 | 0.943 | 0.890 | 0.840 | 0.792 |
| PV of cash flows | ($120,000) | $42,453 | $31,150 | $29,387 | $23,763 |

Present Value of cash flows from Year 1 to Year 4, or 'PVR' = $126,152.19

Present Value of the 'Investment Phase' of the project, or 'PVI' = $120,000

MIRR = $[PVR/PVI]^{1/n} \times (1+re) -1$, where re = the firm's cost of capital.

Here, MIRR = $[\$126,152.19/\$120,000]^{1/4} \times (1+6\%) -1$

MIRR = 7.46%

**153  A**

**154** $5,193.75

|  | $ |
|---|---|
| Salary costs: | |
| Senior consultant 75 hours × $45 | 3,375.00 |
| Junior consultant 30 hours × $26 | 780.00 |
| Marginal cost | 4,155.00 |
| Mark-up (25%) | 1,038.75 |
| | |
| Price to charge client | 5,193.75 |

**155** All items apply, except for the cost of making other unrelated products.

**156 B and E**

A    If demand is very elastic, high market share and a market presence could be achieved quickly by charging a low-penetration pricing.

B    Here market skimming would be more appropriate. A high price could be charged to the 'opinion leaders' who want to be seen to have the new product and are prepared to pay a high price.

C    It is difficult to charge a low price for a product where there are few opportunities for economies of scale since cost per unit will still be high irrespective of production volume.

D    If demand is inelastic, charging a low price will not have a beneficial effect upon sales volume and profit.

E    If there is little competition and high barriers to entry, such as in the pharmaceutical industry, there is no incentive for companies to charge a low price.

**157 B**

At first inspection all four appear to be methods of arriving at selling price.

However, target costing is a method to arrive at the cost at which a product should be produced for having worked backwards from the price already set for the product.

It is a method to arrive at product cost not product selling price.

**158 A**

**159** $70

To maximise profit Maltov must produce where MC = MR (MC is Marginal Cost, MR is Marginal Revenue)

MC = $20                      MR = $120 − Q

So to maximise profit, $20 = $120 − Q

Therefore, Q = $100.

To calculate the price that must be sold, Price = $120 − 0.5 × quantity

So, Price = $120 − 0.5 × $100 = $120 − $50 = $70

**160  C**

$40,000

If components are purchased outside:

| | |
|---|---|
| Contribution earned elsewhere | $25,000 |
| Variable cost saving | $15,000 |
| Maximum price to pay | $40,000 |

**161  C**

The trust is discriminating on the grounds of market segment (segmenting using occupation).

**162**  Marginal cost (MC) = $14

Price (P) = $35 − 0.01q

Marginal Revenue (MR) = $35 − 0.02q

So if MC = MR then:

14 = 35 − 0.02q

0.02q = 21

Q = 1,050

Price = $35 − (0.01 × 1,050)      **= $24.50.**

**163**  $300.

To solve this, we have to derive an equation as follows:

$P$ = price and let $X$ = demand in units

Then

50p = 50,000 − X

$$p = \frac{50,000 - X}{50}$$

p = 1,000 − 0.02X

We are told that the profit maximising level of sales is 35,000 units.

So this is $X$.

Therefore,

p = 1,000 − 0.02 × 35,000 = 1,000 − 700 = $300

**164** The price to set which will maximise profit for 'Samsinging Ltd.' can be found by using a table to calculate the profit resulting for the given price and related sales volumes.

Table for sales levels *per month*

| *Sales quantity* (000 units) | 50 | 100 | 150 | 200 | 250 | 300 | 350 | 400 |
|---|---|---|---|---|---|---|---|---|
| Price per unit ($) | 400 | 375 | 350 | 325 | 300 | 275 | 250 | 225 |
| Revenue ($m) | 20 | 37.5 | 52.5 | 65 | 75 | 82.5 | 87.5 | 90 |
| | | | | | | | | |
| Variable production cost per unit ($) | 240 | 240 | 240 | 240 | 240 | 210 | 210 | 210 |
| Variable production costs ($m) | 12 | 24 | 36 | 48 | 60 | 63 | 73.5 | 84 |
| Fixed production costs ($m) | 4 | 4 | 4 | 4 | 4 | 4.5 | 4.5 | 4.5 |
| Variable selling cost per unit ($) | 35 | 35 | 35 | 40 | 40 | 40 | 40 | 40 |
| Variable selling costs ($m) | 1.75 | 3.5 | 5.25 | 8 | 10 | 12 | 14 | 16 |
| Profit ($m) | 2.25 | 6.0 | 7.25 | 5.0 | 1.0 | 3.0 | (4.5) | (14.5) |

The maximum profit is $7.25 million if 150,000 units are sold at a price of $350 per unit.

So the company should set a selling price of $350 per unit.

**165** Brompton price: Given that the price and volume of sales has been presented as a table, it makes sense to calculate the profit for each piece and quantity combination also using a tabular approach and then select the price at which the level of profit is maximised.

Brompton Ltd wishes to determine the price at which the new toy should be sold in order to maximise profit. A tabular approach can be used as follows:

| Price ($) | 5 | 10 | 15 | 20 | 25 | 30 | 35 | 40 |
|---|---|---|---|---|---|---|---|---|
| Quantity of units (000) | 200 | 180 | 160 | 135 | 120 | 100 | 75 | 50 |
| Sales $000 | 1,000 | 1,800 | 2,400 | 2,700 | 3,000 | 3,000 | 2,625 | 2,000 |
| Variable costs ($6 × no. of units) $000 | 1,200 | 1,080 | 960 | 810 | 720 | 600 | 450 | 300 |
| Fixed costs $000 | 450 | 450 | 450 | 400 | 400 | 400 | 400 | 400 |
| | | | | | | | | |
| Profit/(Loss) | (650) | 270 | 990 | 1,490 | 1,880 | 2,000 | 1,775 | 1,300 |

Profit is maximised when the price is set at $30 per unit. This is therefore the price that should be set by Brompton Ltd.

In order for Electrics Ltd to *maximise profit* it should produce where MC = MR

Since Marginal Cost is the addition to cost of making one more unit, this will be the total variable cost of $600 per unit.

MR is given as MR = 2,000 − 0.02Q, So setting MC = MR gives 600 = 2,000 − 0.02Q

2,000 − 600 = 0.02Q

1,400 = 0.02Q

1,400/0.02 = Q

Therefore, Q = 70,000 units

So in order to maximise profit, Electrics Ltd should produce and sell 70,000 units per annum. The selling price should be:

P = 2,000 − 0.01Q

P = 2,000 − 0.01 × 70,000 = 2,000 − 700 = $1,300

So the selling price in order to maximise profit should be $1,300 per computer.

In order for Electrics Ltd to maximise revenue it should produce where MR = 0

That is, 2,000 − 0.02Q = 0

So 2,000 = 0.02Q

2,000/0.02 = Q

Q = 100,000 units

At a price of P = 2,000 − 0.01Q

P = 2,000 − 0.01 × 100,000

P = 2,000 − 1,000 = $1,000

In order to maximise revenue, Electrics Ltd should produce and sell 100,000 computers at a price of $1,000 per computer.

**166**  **$1,096.36**

The marginal cost and selling price per batch are as follows:

Marginal cost = $672.72

Demand at price of $1,200 = 16 batches and demand increases by 1 unit for every $20 reduction in selling price.

Therefore, Price = $1,520 − 20q          Marginal Revenue = $1,520 − 40q

Equating marginal cost and marginal revenue:

672.72 = 1,520 − 40q                                              40q = 847.28

q = 21.182                                    Price = $1,520 − (20 × 21.182) = **$1,096.36**

**167**  **A**

First find X using MC=MR. Marginal Cost is 25 and the Marginal Revenue function is found from MR =a−2bX or MR=85−0.1X

MC=MR; 25=85−0.1X  Rearrange equation: 0.1X = 85 − 25; 0.1X = 60 so X = 60/0.1 = 600

Revert to demand function P = 85 − (0.05 × 600), so P = 85 − 30 i.e. P= 55

**168**  **C**

**169**  **P**  Profit maximising price

    **a**  Intercept on the y axis (price where sales = zero)

    **b**  Slope of the demand curve

    **X**  Profit Maximising Quantity

**170**  $900

First, we must find the elements of the demand curve: b = 30/150 = 0.2

To find 'a' substitute when Price = zero, demand = 15,000 (where the line cuts the x axis). i.e.

0 = a − (0.2 × 15,000)      0 = a − 3,000      a = 3,000      P = 3000 − 0.2X

And when profit is maximised P = 3,000 − (0.2 × 10,500) = 900

**171**  **C**

B is ALWAYS a negative number. The demand curve always slopes downward (which is why b is always negative). If maximum demand is known it is just another price/demand combination on the demand curve.

**172**  NV (New Vehicle division)

|  | $ |  |
|---|---|---|
| Margin on new vehicle | 8,000 | (40,000 × 20%) |
| Trade in value given | −28,000 |  |
| Transfer price | 16,675 | (17,500 − 825) |
| Total | −3,325 |  |

UV (Used Vehicle division)

|  | $ |
|---|---|
| Sale proceeds | 28,900 |
| Repair costs | −825 |
| Transfer price | −16,675 |
| Total | 11,400 |

VR (Vehicle Repair division)

|  | $ |
|---|---|
| Repairs invoiced | 825 |
| Variable costs | −500 |
| Total | 325 |

XYZ Motor Group

|  | $ |
|---|---|
| NV | −3,325 |
| UV | 11,400 |
| VR | 000325 |
| | ——— |
| Total | 8,400 |
| | ——— |

# D: MANAGEMENT CONTROL AND RISK

## 173   B

Inventing a simple project which fulfils the criteria, for example t0 (1,000), t1 1,100; and revising the t1 cashflow to include 9% inflation rather than 4%, the project becomes:

t0 (1,000), t1 1,153 being (1,100/1.04) × 1.09.

The new internal rate of return is 15.3%.

**Tutorial note**

*Alternatively, you could say the IRR of 10% is a money rate, so our 'real' IRR is 1.10/1.04 − 1 = 5.8%. if inflation changes to 9% then our new money IRR is 1.058 × 1.09 − 1 = 15.3%..*

## 174   D

| Year | Cash | 15% | PV |
|---|---|---|---|
| | $ | | $ |
| 0 | (75,000) | | (75,000) |
| 1 − 5 | 25,000 | 3.352 | 83,800 |
| | | | ——— |
| | | | 8,800 |
| | | | ——— |

Try 20%

| Year | Cash | 20% | PV |
|---|---|---|---|
| | $ | | $ |
| 0 | (75,000) | | (75,000) |
| 1 − 5 | 25,000 | 2.991 | 74,775 |
| | | | ——— |
| | | | (225) |
| | | | ——— |

**175  C**

$$\text{IRR} = 15\% + \frac{8{,}800}{(8{,}800 + 225)} \times 5\%$$

$$\text{IRR} = 15\% + \frac{8{,}800}{9{,}025} \times 5\%$$

$$\text{IRR} = 19.88\%$$

PV of labour cost $= \$20{,}000 \times 3.352$

$= \$67{,}040$

$\therefore$ Allowable change $= \dfrac{8{,}800}{67{,}040} \times 100$  $= \mathbf{13.13\%}$

**176  A**

Sensitivity = NPV/*present value* of the flow under consideration. Therefore, we need the PV of labour costs of $20,000 p.a. for five years, and we can use annuity factor.

$20,000 × 3.791 = $75,820     Sensitivity therefore is 8,800/75,820 =    **11.61%.**

**177  7.93%**

If the present value of the labour costs falls by $7,500 then the project will breakeven.

The PV of the labour costs using annuity factors is 25,000 × 3.784 = 94,600

Therefore 7,500/94,600 =    **7.93%**

**178  D**

Sensitivity analysis can only show the impact of a cash flow changing, but not the likelihood.

**179  B**

Expected annual cash flow : 30 × 0.3 + 35 × 0.5 + 45 × 0.2 = $35.5 × 10,000 units = $355,000

Present value of $355,000 per annum – use 12% annuity factor of 3.605

$355,000 × 3.605 = $1,279,775

If you chose A you didn't round as the question asked. If you chose C, you used a discount factor not an annuity factor. If you chose D, you just calculated the single year cash flow and didn't discount.

**180** $8,834

| Cash flows | Probability | Year 1 | Year 2 |
|---|---|---|---|
| Optimistic | 0.3 × 70,000 | = 21,000 | |
| | 0.3 × 85,000 | | = 25,500 |
| Most likely | 0.45 × 40,000 | = 18,000 | |
| | 0.45 × 55,000 | | = 24,750 |
| Pessimistic | 0.25 × 25,000 | = 6,250 | |
| | 0.25 × 30,000 | | = 7,500 |
| Total flow | | **$45,250** | **$57,750** |

**NPV**

| Time | Cash flow | Discount factor | Present Value |
|---|---|---|---|
| 0 | (80,000) | 1 | (80,000) |
| 1 | 45,250 | 0.909 | 41,132 |
| 2 | 57,750 | 0.826 | 47702 |
| NPV | | | **$8,834** |

**181 A**

Contribution at today's prices = 4,000 × $5 = $20,000. This increases by 3% per annum.

| Year | Money cash | Discount at 8% | Present value |
|---|---|---|---|
| 0 | $(50,000) | | $(50,000) |
| 1 | $20,600 | 0.926 | $19,076 |
| 2 | $21,218 | 0.857 | $18,184 |
| 3 | $21,855 | 0.794 | $17,353 |
| | | | **$4,613** |

**182 C**

Inflation is now 4%. Continuing to work in money cash:

| Year | Money cash | Try 14% | Present value |
|---|---|---|---|
| 0 | $(50,000) | | $(50,000) |
| 1 | $20,800 | 0.877 | $18,242 |
| 2 | $21,632 | 0.769 | $16,635 |
| 3 | $22,497 | 0.675 | $15,185 |
| | | | **$62** |

An NPV of $62 is virtually zero. Discounting at 14.5% would reduce the NPV by several hundred pounds. Therefore, the maximum monetary cost for the project to remain viable is 14%.

**183  A**

| Annual contribution | = annual cash profit + annual cash fixed costs | |
|---|---|---|
| | = \$450,000 + \$190,000 | = \$640,000 |
| Contribution/unit | = \$220 − \$55 | = \$165 |
| ∴ Units sold pa | = \$640,000 ÷ \$165 | = 3,879 units. |

The NPV of the project can fall by \$127,600 before it becomes zero.

The NPV of total annual revenue is expected to be 3,879 × \$220 × 4.623  = \$3,945,175.

For this to fall by \$127,600, it must suffer a decrease of $\dfrac{127,600}{3,945,175}$ × 100% = 3.2%

**184  A**

The present value of expected sales revenue is as follows:

| Year | Item | Cash flow | Discount factor at 10% | PV |
|---|---|---|---|---|
| | | \$ | | \$ |
| 1 | Sales revenue | 40,000 | 0.909 | 36,360 |
| 2 | Sales revenue | 40,000 | 0.826 | 33,040 |
| 3 | Sales revenue | 24,000 | 0.751 | 18,024 |
| NPV | | | | 87,424 |

The NPV is \$3,190, so the maximum reduction in sales price that can occur without the project ceasing to be viable is (3,190/87,424) = 0.036 = 3.6%.

**185  B**

The present value of the annual net cash flows, ignoring the machine cost and residual value, is: \$(19,998 + 18,172 + 7,510) = \$45,680.

If the machine costs \$X, the net cost of the machine, in present value terms and allowing for the residual value at the end of year 3, is:

X − (0.751 × 20% of X)

= X − 0.1502X

= 0.8498X.

If 0.8498X exceeds \$45,680, the project will not be viable. The maximum amount the machine can cost without the project ceasing to be viable is therefore \$45,680/0.8498 = \$53,754, say \$54,000.

**186  C**

Sensitivity = NPV of project/PV of figures which vary = \$320,000/\$630,000 = 51%

**187**

| Year | Cash | 15% | PV |
|------|------|-----|-----|
| | $ | | $ |
| 0 | (75,000) | | (75,000) |
| 1 – 5 | 25,000 | 3.352 | 83,800 |
| | | | 8,800 |

Try 20%

| Year | Cash | 20% | PV |
|------|------|-----|-----|
| | $ | | $ |
| 0 | (75,000) | | (75,000) |
| 1 – 5 | 25,000 | 2.991 | 74,775 |
| | | | (225) |

$$\text{IRR} = 15\% + \frac{8,800}{(8,800+225)} \times 5\%$$

$$\text{IRR} = 15\% + \frac{8,800}{9,025} \times 5\%$$

$$\text{IRR} = 19.88\%$$

$$\text{PV of labour cost} = \$20,000 \times 3.352$$
$$= \$67,040$$
$$\therefore \text{ Allowable change} = \frac{8,800}{67,040} \times 100$$
$$= 13.13\%$$

**188**  7.8%

| Year | Discount factor | Increase in cost ($000) | Present value ($000) | Savings ($000) | Present value ($000) |
|------|------|------|------|------|------|
| 1 | 0.833 | 16 | 13.328 | 150 | 124.95 |
| 2 | 0.694 | 20 | 13.880 | 160 | 111.04 |
| 3 | 0.579 | 24 | 13.896 | 170 | 98.43 |
| 4 | 0.482 | 30 | 14.460 | 180 | 86.76 |
| | | | 55.564 | | 421.18 |

The Present Value of costs increases by $55,564; this means that NPV falls to $22,900 − $55,564 = − $32,664. Therefore, the present value of savings must rise by $32,664, or $\frac{32,664}{421,180} \times 100 = 7.8\%$.

**189** C series for the pessimistic buyer; A series for the optimistic buyer, as the best possible result comes from getting a 'grade A' truck. C series for the buyer prone to regretting decisions (see regret table below) and C series for the risk neutral buyer, based on Expected Values calculations (see below.)

| Regret table | | Type of truck | | |
|---|---|---|---|---|
| | | **A grade** | **B grade** | **C grade** |
| Growth rate | 15% | 1,200 | 1,800 | 0 |
| | 30% | 3,100 | 2,600 | 0 |
| | 40% | 0 | 2,100 | 1,000 |
| Max regret | | 3,100 | 2,600 | 1,000 |

Expected value calculations:

A Grade: $(2,400 \times 0.4) + (1,400 \times 0.25) + (4,900 \times 0.35) = 3,025$

B Grade: $(1,800 \times 0.4) + (1,900 \times 0.25) + (2,800 \times 0.35) = 2,175$

C Grade: $(3,600 \times 0.4) + (4,500 \times 0.25) + (3,900 \times 0.35) = 3,930$

**190** The third point did not apply. The following do apply:

- ◯ Simulation models the behaviour of a system
- ◯ Simulation models can be used to study alternative solutions to a problem.
- ◯ A simulation model cannot prescribe what should be done about a problem.

**191 B**

Without information, the expected profits are:

Product X: $\$20,000 \times 0.2 + \$15,000 \times 0.5 + \$6,000 \times 0.3 \quad = \quad \$13,300$

Product Y: $\$17,000 \times 0.2 + \$16,000 \times 0.5 + \$7,000 \times 0.3 \quad = \quad \$13,500$

So without information, product Y would be selected.

With perfect information, product X would be selected if the market was good, and product Y in the other two cases. The expected value would then be:

$\$20,000 \times 0.2 + \$16,000 \times 0.5 + \$7,000 \times 0.3 = \$14,100$

The expected value of perfect information is therefore $\$14,100 - \$13,500 = \$600$

**192**

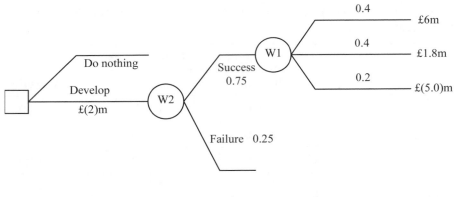

(W1) EV  =  $6m × 0.4 + $1.8m × 0.4 − $5m × 0.2

=  $2.12m

(W2) EV  =  $2.12m × 0.75 + $0 × 0.25

=  $1.59m

Net benefit: $1.59m − $2m

=  ($0.41)m

**193  A**

| | |
|---|---|
| Additional sales 60 boxes × ($3 selling price − $2 cost) | $60 |
| And unsold 40 boxes × ($1 selling price − $2 cost) | $(40) |
| Profit | $20 |
| Probability | × 0.6 |
| Expected value | $12 |
| | |
| Additional sales 100 boxes × ($3 selling price − $2 cost) | $100 |
| And unsold 0 boxes × ($1 selling price) | $0 |
| Profit | $100 |
| Probability | × 0.4 |
| Expected profit | $40 |
| | |
| Expected profit (value) of decision | **$52** |

**194  A**

Most probability problems have you compute the expected value from a series of possible outcomes, each weighted with its own likelihood of occurrence. However, in this problem, the company only wants to select the most likely sales volume figure. That would be the one with the greatest probability of occurrence.

**195  A**

| Selling price | x | Probability of selling price | = | Expected value |
|---|---|---|---|---|
| $5,000 | | 40% | | $2,000 |
| $8,000 | | 20% | | $1,600 |
| $12,000 | | 30% | | $3,600 |
| $30,000 | | 10% | | $3,000 |
| **Expected selling price** | | | **=** | **$10,200** |

**196  A**

The probability of the lead time being 3 days is 25%, and the probability of demand being 3 units in a day is 10%. The probability of 3 days of demand being 3 units (3 × 3 = 9) coupled with a 3-day lead time is as follows: 0.25 × 0.1 × 0.1 × 0.1 = 0.00025

**197  E**

| Forecast | Actual sales | | |
|---|---|---|---|
| | *High* | *Low* | |
| High | 0.5525 | 0.0525 | 0.605 |
| Low | 0.0975 | 0.2975 | 0.395 |
| | 0.65 | 0.35 | 1.00 |

Probability = 0.0975/0.395 = 0.2468

**198**  Using 1,000 as a suitable multiple, i.e. considering 1,000 cakes are baked, the contingency table is:

| | Made at factory | | |
|---|---|---|---|
| | *X* | *Y* | *Total* |
| Has not been baked properly | 30 | 84 | 114 |
| Has been baked properly | 270 | 616 | 886 |
| Total | 300 | 700 | 1,000 |

Therefore, P (Made in bakery B/not baked properly) = 84/114 = 0.737 or 73.7%

## 199   RECYC

### Payoff table

| | | Level of waste | | |
|---|---|---|---|---|
| | | High | Medium | Low |
| Advance | High | 962.5 | 636.5 | 397.5 |
| order of | Medium | 912.5 | 655.5 | 442.5 |
| chemical | Low | 837.5 | 617.5 | 457.5 |

### (W1)

| Advance order of chemical X | Level of waste | Prob. | Contrib. (excl. X) (W2) $000 | Chemical X cost (W3) $000 | Net contribution $000 |
|---|---|---|---|---|---|
| High | High | 0.30 | 1,462.5 | 500 | 962.5 |
| | Medium | 0.50 | 1,111.5 | 475 | 636.5 |
| | Low | 0.20 | 877.5 | 480 | 397.5 |
| Medium | High | 0.30 | 1,462.5 | 550 | 912.5 |
| | Medium | 0.50 | 1,111.5 | 456 | 655.5 |
| | Low | 0.20 | 877.5 | 435 | 442.5 |
| Low | High | 0.30 | 1,462.5 | 625 | 837.5 |
| | Medium | 0.50 | 1,111.5 | 494 | 617.5 |
| | Low | 0.20 | 877.5 | 420 | 457.5 |

### (W2)  Waste available

| | High | Medium | Low |
|---|---|---|---|
| Aluminium extracted (000 kg) | 7,500 | 5,700 | 4,500 |
| | $000 | $000 | $000 |
| Sales revenue (at $0.65 per kg) | 4,875.0 | 3,705.0 | 2,925.0 |
| Variable cost (at 70%) | 3,412.5 | 2,593.5 | 2,047.5 |
| Contribution | 1,462.5 | 1,111.5 | 877.5 |

Maximax suggests that the decision maker should look for the largest possible profit from all the outcomes. In this case this is a high advance order of chemical X where there is a possibility of a contribution of $962,500. This indicates a risk seeking preference by management. Although it offers the possibility of the highest contribution, there is also a 20% likelihood that the worst outcome of $397,500 will occur.

Maximin suggests that the decision maker should look for the strategy which maximises the minimum possible contribution. In this case this is a low advance order of chemical X where the lowest contribution is $457,500. This is better than the worst possible outcomes from high or medium advance orders of chemical X. This indicates a risk-averse management posture.

### (W3)  Examples of workings for chemical X cost

- High advance level of order for chemical X and low actual requirement: The price of $1.00 is subject to a penalty of $0.60 per kg. The cost of chemical X is, therefore, 300,000 kg × $1.60 = $480,000

- Low advance level of order for chemical X and medium actual requirement: The price is subject to a discount of $0.10 per kg. The cost of chemical X is, therefore, 380,000 × $1.30 = $494,000.

## 200 TICKET AGENT

(a) The question specifies that a long-run perspective is being taken so decisions can be made by reference to expected values.

**Expected sales demand**

|  | Probability | Demand | EV |
|---|---|---|---|
| Popular artistes | 0.45 | 500 | 225 |
| Lesser known artistes | 0.30 | 350 | 105 |
| Unknown artistes | 0.25 | 200 | 50 |
|  |  |  | 380 |

Expected demand = 380 tickets per concert

Maximising profit

To determine the best decision, the expected profits for each possible order level need to be calculated.

- Payoff table showing profit (W1, W2)

|  |  | Actual sales demand | | |
|---|---|---|---|---|
|  |  | 200 | 350 | 500 |
|  | 200 | 1,200 | 1,200 | 1,200 |
| Purchase | 300 | (570) | 2,250 | 2,250 |
| Level | 400 | (2,040) | 2,190 | 3,600 |
|  | 500 | (2,460) | 1,770 | 6,000 |

- Expected values

|  |  | EV |
|---|---|---|
| 200 tickets | $1,200 \times 1$ | 1,200 |
| 300 tickets | $(570) \times 0.25 + 2,250 \times 0.75$ | 1,545 |
| 400 tickets | $(2,040) \times 0.25 + 2,190 \times 0.3 + 3,600 \times 0.45$ | 1,767 |
| 500 tickets | $(2,460) \times 0.25 + 1,770 \times 0.3 + 6,000 \times 0.45$ | 2,616 |

**The optimum purchase level** is 500 tickets per concert, which will give an expected profit of $2,616 per concert.

**Workings**

(W1) The gross profit made per ticket is the discount received on the selling price of $30.

| Purchase level | Discount |  |  | Profit per ticket sold |
|---|---|---|---|---|
| 200 | 20% | 20% × $30 | = | $6.00 |
| 300 | 25% | 25% × $30 | = | $7.50 |
| 400 | 30% | 30% × $30 | = | $9.00 |
| 500 | 40% | 40% × $30 | = | $12.00 |

(W2) Each net profit calculation consists of up to three elements:

1 the profit on the units sold

2 the cost of the units which are unsold and returned

3 the value of the returns

EV of returns = $30.00 × 60% × 10% = $1.80 per return.

Example calculation:

Buy 300 tickets but can only sell 200 ⇒ Sell 200 tickets and return 100 tickets

|  | $ |
|---|---|
| Sales 200 tickets × 7.50 (W1) | 1,500 |
| EV of returns 100 tickets × $1.80 | 180 |
|  | 1,680 |
| Cost of returns 100 tickets × $22.50 (25% discount) | (2,250) |
|  | (570) |

(b)   **Maximax**

The agent should order 500 tickets as this gives a maximum possible gain of $6,000 per concert.

**Maximin**

The agent should buy 200 tickets to maximise the minimum possible pay-off ($1,200).

**Minimax regret**

A regret table is found by comparing the actual profit with what could have been made given the level of demand that occurred:

|  |  | Actual sales demand | | |
|---|---|---|---|---|
|  |  | 200 | 350 | 500 |
|  | 200 | 0 | 1,050 | 4,800 |
| Purchase | 300 | 1,770 | 0 | 3,750 |
| Level | 400 | 3,240 | 60 | 2,400 |
|  | 500 | 3,660 | 480 | 0 |

The agent would thus order 400 tickets as this limits the maximum regret to $3,240.

This level of order would give an average profit of $1,767 per concert.

## 201   SHIFTERS HAULAGE

**Profit calculations**

|  | Small van | Medium van | Large van |
|---|---|---|---|
| Capacity | 100 | 150 | 200 |
| Low Demand (120) | 300 (W1) | 468 (W3) | 368 (W5) |
| High Demand (190) | 300 (W2) | 500 (W4) | 816 (W6) |

| **Workings** | (W1) | (W2) | (W3) | (W4) | (W5) | (W6) |
|---|---|---|---|---|---|---|
| Sales | 1,000 | 1,000 | 1,200 | 1,500 | 1,200 | 1,900 |
| VC | (400) | (400) | (480) | (600) | (480) | (760) |
| Goodwill | (100) | (100) |  | (100) |  |  |
| VC adjustment |  |  | 48 |  | 48 | 76 |
| Depreciation | (200) | (200) | (300) | (300) | (400) | (400) |
| Profit | 300 | 300 | 468 | 500 | 368 | 816 |

## 202   COOL SYSTEMS

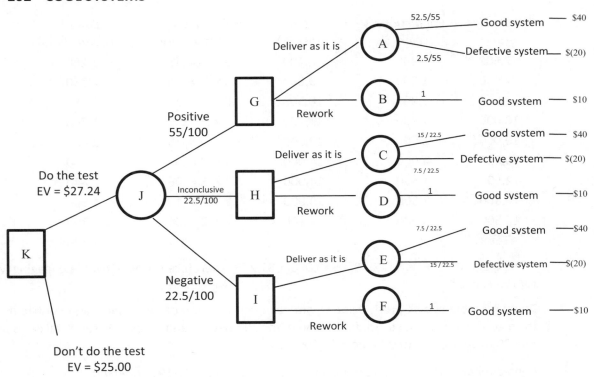

EV(A) = [(52.5/55) × $40)] − [(2.5/55)X $20)] = $37.27

EV(B) = $10

So our choice at 'G' will be to **deliver the system as it is**.

EV(C) = EV(E) = [(15/22.5)  ×  $40)] − [(7.5/22.5)X $20)] = $20

EV(D) = $10

So our choice at 'H' will be to **deliver the system as it is**.

EV(E) = [(7.5/22.5)  ×  $40)] − [(15/22.5)X $20)] = $0

EV(F) = $10

So our choice at 'I' will be to **rework the system**.

EV(J) = (0.55X $37.27) + (0.225X$20) + (0.225 × $10) = $27.24

Therefore EV of Imperfect Information: $27.24 − $25.00 = $2.24

## 203  THEATRE

| Ticket sales ($) | Confectionary sales ($) | Total sales ($) | Joint × probability | Sales × probability ($) |
|---|---|---|---|---|
| 7,500 | 900 | 8,400 | .5 × .3 = .15 | 1,260 |
| 7,500 | 1,500 | 9,000 | .5 × .5 = .25 | 2,250 |
| 7,500 | 3,000 | 10,500 | .5 × .2 = .10 | 1,050 |
| 10,000 | 1,200 | 11,200 | .3 × .3 = .09 | 1,008 |
| 10,000 | 2,000 | 12,000 | .3 × .5 = .15 | 1,800 |
| 10,000 | 4,000 | 14,000 | .3 × .2 = .06 | 840 |
| 12,500 | 1,500 | 14,000 | .2 × .3 = .06 | 840 |
| 12,500 | 2,500 | 15,000 | .2 × .5 = .10 | 1,500 |
| 12,500 | 5,000 | 17,500 | .2 × .2 = .04 | 700 |
| Total | | | 1.00 | 11,248 |

The expected value is $11,248 − $10,000 = $1,248. Therefore it is worthwhile engaging MS for the concert.

The data table shows profit values from each combination of ticket sales and contribution from confectionary sales. So, for example, for 300 people and $3 per person total sales are $8,400 (from (a)) − $10,000 fee = $1,600 loss.

| Confectionary sales | $3 per person | $5 per person | $10 per person |
|---|---|---|---|
| Ticket sales | | | |
| 300 people | (1,600) | (1,000) | 500 |
| 400 people | 1,200 | 2,000 | 4,000 |
| 500 people | 4,000 | 5,000 | 7,500 |

## 204  AMELIE

In order to decide whether or not to hire the consultant, expected valued for decision alternatives are calculated, starting on the right hand side of the tree and moving leftwards (backtracking).

At node D:

EV(I) = (0 .9 * $30,000) − (0 .1 *$10,000) = $26,000

EV(J) = (0 .9 * $60,000) − (0 .1 *$40,000) = $50,000

EV(K) = (0 .9 * $0) − (0 .1 *$0) = $0

So, the decision at Node D should be to go for a large shop, as the EV of outcome J is the highest of the three possible decisions I, J and K.

At node E :

EV(L) = (0 .12 * $30,000) − (0 .88 *$10,000) = ($5,200)

EV(M) = (0 .12 * $60,000) − (0 .88 *$40,000) = ($28,000)

EV(N) = (0 .12 * $0) − (0 .88 *$0) = $0

So, the decision at Node E should be not to go for any shop at all, as the EV of outcome N is the only non-loss making option.

At node C:

EV(F) = (0 .5 * $30,000) – (0 .5 *$10,000) = $10,000

EV(G) = (0 .5 * $60,000) – (0 .5 *$40,000) = $10,000

EV(H) = (0 .5 * $0) – (0 .5 *$0) = $0

So, the decision at Node C should be to go for either a small or a large shop, as both offer the same positive EV of a profit.

To decide between hiring a consultant at $5,000 and not hiring a consultant, we need to calculate the EV of profits at node B:

EV (B) = (0.6 × $50,000) + (0 .4 × $0) = $30,000

Therefore, profits if a consultant is hired are expected to reach

$30,000 – cost of research $5,000 = $25,000

EV (C) = $10,000, if no market research is undertaken. The expected value of profits is higher if market research is undertaken, therefore Amelie should hire the consultant.

- We first need to calculate what the expected value of profits with perfect information would be. If the second consultant predicts a favourable cheese market (0.6 probability), we should opt for a large shop and obtain $60,000 profit. If the consultant predicts an unfavourable market, we should not go for no shop at all (and profits will be nil.)

  Therefore EV of profits with perfect information = 0.6 × $60,000 + (0 × $0)

  = $36,000

  Expected profit with imperfect market research information from first consultant

  = $25,000

  Value of perfect information = $11,000

**205 C**

Valorisation

**206** Big Data management involves using sophisticated systems to gather, store and analyse large volumes of data in a variety of structured and unstructured formats. In addition to traditional data from internal sources such as sales history, preferences, order frequency and pricing information, companies can also gather information from external sources such as websites, trade publications and social networks. Collating and analysing these large volumes of information allows companies to gain a variety of insights into customer behaviour and this can help to more accurately predict customer demand. These demand forecasts may be in terms of volume but also the type of products required and this is beneficial to company planning but can also help the company to improve aspects of the customer experience. In terms of volume predictions, these can help to ensure that a company will always have sufficient inventory to satisfy demand. This will mean that customers do not need to wait to receive their goods which is likely to be a key part of their shopping experience. Furthermore companies can use the information and insights to understand which products and features are most popular with customers. This can inform product re-design to ensure that any revisions are in line with customer preferences.

**207** Business data can be difficult to manage for a variety of reasons and these can be summarised using the 3 V's of velocity, volume and variety.

**Velocity**

The speed at which data is now generated from sources such as social media networks makes it incredibly difficult for traditional database management systems to cope and give relevant and timely insights. If this data is not managed effectively it is, at best, wasted but could also result in significant increases in the data storage capacity required, without seeing any particular benefits.

**Volume**

Companies can now gather and generate data from a huge range of sources including internal systems, e-commerce sources, competitor and customer websites and social media networks. Not only has the overall volume of sources increased but the amount of data gathered from each source is now much higher than from traditional reporting. For example the data gathered from a single e-commerce sales transaction can be up to ten times higher than a standard in-store transaction. It is important that data is only gathered (and therefore stored and analysed) from relevant sources that can actually add value to company decision making as there is a danger that companies become obsessed with gathering all data that is available rather than just that which is useful.

**Variety**

An increasing number of incompatible and inconsistent data formats is emerging at a fast rate. Most traditional data management systems are based around extracting data from, and storing data in, standard formats such as XML. Collecting data in a wide variety of formats including sound files and GPS data creates challenges for a system managing such big data.

**208** A

**209** B

**210** D

**211** C

**212** B

The following information is given by the question:

(i)     There are 100 students in total.

(ii)    30 students are male (hence 100 − 30 = 70 are female).

(iii)   55 students are studying for Certificate Stage (hence 100 − 55 = 45 are not studying for Certificate Stage).

(iv)    6 male students are not studying (hence 30 − 6 = 24 are studying).

For simplicity this information can be placed into a table.

|  | *Not studying* | *Studying* | *Total* |
|---|---|---|---|
| Male | 6 | (30 − 6) = 24 | 30 |
| Female | (45 − 6) = 39 | (70 − 39) = 31 | 70 |
| Total | 45 | 55 | 100 |

The probability that a randomly chosen female student is not studying is $\dfrac{39}{70}$,

i.e. P(NS/F) = 0.56.

**213** The probability that a randomly-selected brand x buyer is from the north and under 25 years of age is (to 2 decimal places):

$$P = \boxed{0.08}$$

The probability that a randomly-selected Brand X buyer is from the West or under 25 years of age is (to 2 decimal places):

$$P = \boxed{0.48}$$

The probability that a randomly-selected Brand X buyer, who is under 25 years of age, is from the South is (to 3 decimal places):

$$P = \boxed{0.375}$$

The probability that two randomly-selected Brand X buyers are both under 25 years of age is (to two decimal places):

$$P = \boxed{0.09}$$

**Workings**

(i)   Probability = 400/5,200 = 0.769 = 0.08

(ii)  West buyers          = 1,300

      Under 25s            = 1,600

      West and under 25    = 400

      West or under 25     = 1,300 + 1,600 − 400

                           = 2,500

      Probability          = 2,500/5,200

                           = 0.48

(iii) Probability   = 600/1,600 = 0.375

(iv)  Probability   = 1,600/5,200 × 1,599/5,199 = 0.0946 = 0.09